The Norfolk Library

I WALKED BY NIGHT

I
WALKED
BY
NIGHT

Being the Life & History of
the King of the Norfolk Poachers

WRITTEN BY

HIMSELF

EDITED BY

LILIAS RIDER HAGGARD

ILLUSTRATED BY

EDWARD SEAGO

BOYDELL PRESS
WAVENEY PUBLICATIONS

Published by The Boydell Press
an imprint of Boydell & Brewer Ltd
PO Box 9, Woodbridge,
Suffolk IP12 3DF
in association with Waveney Publications
Ditchingham Lodge, Bungay, Suffolk

First published 1935
Reprinted in The Norfolk Library 1974
Reprinted 1975, 1976, 1977, 1978, 1981, 1991

ISBN   0 85115 046 2

Printed in Great Britain by
St Edmundsbury Press, Bury St Edmunds, Suffolk

PREFACE

WHAT is written here was born of an old man's loneliness, as he sat in a little cottage perched high on a hill, overlooking the Waveney Valley with no company but his dog. The life that he loved had passed him by. As he puts it, 'some said I had given up the game—but the game gave me up', so to pass the time he took to writing down his memories in a penny exercise-book. Subsequently it was handed over to amuse a farmer friend of mine, one day when times were bad with the author, and he had come up to see if there was job for him 'mole catchen'.

To the farmer's wife I am indebted for the fact that two years later it came into my hands: knowing that I 'had a fancy for such things' she had pushed it into a drawer to await the day when I came in. The dog-eared and grimy pages of that exercise-book proved my first introduction to the history of the King of the Norfolk Poachers, but not to its author.

For many years he had been something of a local celebrity, and had appeared with great regularity before my father on two local Benches. The sound of his gun was also familiar in our ears. He still mourns the fact that he hooked off one of his illuminated 'sites' on the wire netting of our shrubbery, and lost it in the long grass, 'where as like as not it lie to this day'. Once, and not so many years ago, I unwittingly delivered him into the hands of the unsympathetic law myself, his pocket bulging with three pheasants; but that I have not confessed to him. I was endeavouring to ensnare the butler and gardener of one of our tenants, and caught the wrong bird, but since have had reason to think that they were all 'in the firm' together with a donkey-cart. But I must desist lest I grow too personal.

The fact that it is not possible to regain the town of Bungay from the Norfolk side except by crossing one narrow bridge on the outskirts (unless one takes a detour of some miles, or crosses the river in a boat) has been the undoing of many a night walker who desired his perambulations unnoticed. Wait on the bridge and you have them sooner or later. That is what on this occasion the police, warned by me, had done.

The farmer's wife only half approved of the old man and his literary efforts, partly because her innate respectability was outraged at his reputation, and partly from an inborn distrust of one who had mysteriously cured her son of warts when all other remedies had failed. Had she not spent more than enough upon the chemist's nostrums, with no result, until one day, when singling beet, the old poacher's eye fell on the boy's hands. He dealt with the warts and they vanished with no further ado; but the boy's mother was a Londoner, and did not hold with such ideas as 'charming', which to those who dwell in East Anglia seems to this day a most rational remedy. Still she was a kindly soul, and cherished a soft spot for the charmer, even after reading the shocking revelations set forth in the exercise-book.

As for myself, I saw that there was more to be had from him than the impish pleasure of an old man in the memories of his lawlessness. Over many months I collected what is set down in this book. It is entirely his own work, but it was not written as it appears here, as it was in no way consecutive. It came to me in letters and on scraps of paper, in old exercise-books, on anything that was at hand when answering some random question of mine. Sometimes, like a water diviner, I hit the spring and the twig twitched; at others it was a case of 'no contact'. He had, however—which helped me enormously—a vivid remembrance of his young days and a natural love of writing. He says himself: 'At times wen I gets the pen into my hand I feel I could go on for ever, old scenes, old faces, old memries come back into my mind, of the days wen I was young'. The strength of those memories may be judged by the fact that it was with the greatest reluctance he would tell me much of the days he spent with his much-loved first wife—even now I do not know her name.

I have done but little pruning; most of my work has been arrangement of material so as to make the book a narrative, with the incidents in their right places. Also such minor services to the MS. as punctuation and some revision of spelling, although much has been left exactly as he wrote it. The Ballads are largely his. These are of interest, as I do not think that most of them will be found in any collection. They are not of the same class as many of the traditional ballads which come down from very early times, but are entirely rural, and, I should imagine, much later in date. I cannot do better than quote his own comment on them:

'There are a lot of the old songs that I know, songs that my Grandmother and Mother lerned me wen I was a Child, songs that had been rote more than a hundred years ago. It must have been so, as my Grandparents lerned them wen they were young, and they have been dead more than fifty year. My Mother and Grandmother were singers in there younger days and had good voices, but of corse other Old People knew those songs as well. They were the songs that were sung at harvest Homes, and some of them were rather rude and vulger, or would be thought so now, but the words of the song in them days was little thought on, if the musick were new. I could perhaps rite you a dozen or more of those old songs—there were mostly a murder in them, and some were rather Comick perhaps. I have never seen any of those old songs in print, and they are mostley forgoten now. If you would care for any of them, I should be onley to pleased to rite them for you.'

Some proved too fragmentary to use, but the ones which appear in this book had only to have an occasional missing rhyme supplied, or extra lines deleted because of repetition and length.

I have let some paragraphs in the book stand which might, for various reasons, have been cut. My object was that those who read it might see the writer as he is (not as I might romantically have imagined him), with all his obvious crudities of opinion and strange code of honour. You must have lived long among the people of East Anglia to understand at all some of his points of view. They are a strange people 'born of the East Wind', as my father used to tell me: slow, intensely suspicious of strangers (you remain one for at least thirty years after arrival in these parts), and often possessing a curious twist of mind. But if they are bitter and long of memory in their hatreds, they are equally stubborn, generous, and courageous in their allegiance, whether it be to person, place, or custom. There is a theory that their typical characteristics were evolved owing to the centuries of periodic invasion and persecution which East Anglia suffered at the hands of Roman, Saxon, and Dane, for close on a thousand years, before the country settled down after the Norman Conquest.

To compile this book has been a labour of love, partly because it is so essentially 'Norfolk', and partly, perhaps, because an old man very much like the author was the constant companion of my childhood. He lived on the estate, in a tumble-down old mill-house on the river, and was the source of innumerable delights. He built boats, he kept ferrets, he knew all the ways of bird and beast. He was an inveterate poacher, and taught my boy cousins how to nab the unwary cock pheasant, which they did with mingled joy and terror, persuaded thereto by the urgent, husky, and mysterious whisper which was his habitual mode of speech. A speech which was entirely unintelligible to any but his intimates. He used also to trap eels, and, greatest joy of all, taught us how to eel-bab.

I have ceased to go eel-babbing. Since the old man went to the Happy Hunting Grounds no one near at hand will make the babs—particularly noisome objects, consisting of large earth-worms soaked in some noxious mixture of cow dung, threaded with red wool (to entangle the eel's teeth) and tied together in large bunches at the end of a short line fastened to a hazel twig. I can, however, still enjoy it second-hand. My house lies in the cup of the wooded slopes which enclose the Waveney Valley, and Bungay, or Outney Common, to give it its proper name, with its great expanse of marsh and heath, stretches out before my windows, and away into the distance towards Beccles and the sea.

On certain still hot nights in summer, when the wind is in the south and the moon rises late, the eel-babbers come to the Common side of the river which runs at the foot of my garden, and is the boundary between the counties of Norfolk and Suffolk. Very quiet it is then. Sandpiper, plover, and strong flighting swans are gone with the tumult of spring. The voice of the frogs and the continuous quivering drum of the nesting snipe have fallen silent. Later on the owls will begin their autumn chorus, but now only the chatter and creak of the reed bunting sounds through the warm dark. As I lie in bed I can hear the muted voices of the babbers as they lower the bunches of worms gently on to the mud shallows beloved by the eels, and the occasional 'plop' of a fat one as he is dropped into the tin bath they carry with them. At last, about midnight, when the mist, which has been lying in long lines over the dykes, rises breast high and spreads a veil of mystery over the marshes, they gather up their spoils and set off on the mile-and-a-half walk back to Bungay.

It was to this part of the world that the old poacher came in his latter days, and from his point of view it was a well-chosen habitation. The valley here lies like a great saucer, and the river Waveney, leaving its direct course at Bungay, encircles the whole of Outney Common and marshes in a vast loop, returning to Bungay again, the town being built on higher ground in the neck of the loop. All round the valley are low hills, alternately wooded and rough pasture-land. Shoot runs into shoot; Ellingham just beyond Bungay, then Ditchingham and Earsham on the loop, and beyond that the great expanse of the Flixton Woods, running up the river to Homersfield and beyond.

Hares, rabbits, pheasants, and partridges abound, and at certain seasons plover, wild duck, woodcock, and snipe come in to feed in varying numbers. A further convenience for the Poacher exists in the fact that the valley woods are mostly far from any road, and behind my house, and all along the top of the slope, runs an ancient right-of-way, partly bridle-path, partly a disused highway, so it is possible for anyone to pass right through the centre of the different properties unquestioned and unhindered. If by any chance the land path is unhealthy, a boat on the river is handy, which can slip silently either up or down stream to Bungay town.

I also know the north-west of Norfolk which figures so largely in the

early part of this book, for it is the country of my father's people. I was
very lately in Pentney—the author's home for so many years. It is still a
place of wide fields, great gorse-covered commons and stretches of fen,
full-bosomed with reed and black water, lying desolate and stirless under
the sky. The pound and the poacher's old cottage are gone; only the
apple trees remain to mark where it once stood, leaning wearily over a
tangle of brambles and nettles which cover what was once his garden,
and the path so jealously guarded by the dogs.

All that part of Norfolk is singularly untouched by the desirable but
often nightmare passage of progress. The many-wintered woods, rambling
farm-houses, and storied barns stand unchanged, safely cradled in the
sunlit fields, outposts of Georgian hall and mellow Elizabethan manor.
Some have shuttered windows like blind eyes, dimmed with gazing for a
future which should restore their past prosperity. But they stand isolated
amidst their parks, with still no hint of the sprawling growths of the
speculative builder creeping ever nearer to their gates.

Go through the little town of Dereham on market day, when the
brightly coloured and variously laden stalls are jostling each other out
into the middle of the wide street, so picturesquely flanked with gracious
many-windowed Georgian houses and steep dormered little shops. The
crowd you push your way through is different to what you will see
even in the south of the county. I have a shrewd idea it is the same in
almost every detail of appearance, speech, manner, and thought as the
crowd my great-grandfather rode through on market days a good
hundred years ago.

I hold no brief for a stagnant world. I have seen too much of the bitter
fruit of ignorance and apathy in country places. 'Enlightenment', as our
author has it, must come, and its banners go before in the shape of
advertisement hoardings and cheap literature. There is, however, a
breadth, a simplicity and an unhurried dignity about life in these remote
villages, which are even yet untouched by the motor bus, the cinema,
and the summer visitor.

This book is an authentic picture of such places, and of the life of an age fast vanishing under more modern conditions. My hope is that some who love the country and its people as they really are—not as some writers would have us believe they are—will find pleasure in reading it. Also that beneath some portions which are commonplace they will find others which touch a deeper truth, a truth and a wisdom which are found in such widely differing minds.

I have touched not at all on the story contained in these pages—the author tells it quite completely for himself. I can only assure all who read it that it is his story as he intended it, not altered nor distorted in any fashion.

LILIAS RIDER HAGGARD

DITCHINGHAM, NORFOLK
May 1935

THE MAN OF DOUBLE DEED

There was a Man of Double Deed
Who sowed his Garden full of Seed,
And when the Seed began to grow
'Twas like a Garden full of Snow,
And when the Snow began to melt
'Twas like a Shoe without a Welt,
And when the Shoe began to sail
'Twas like a Bird without a Tail,
And when the Bird began to fly
'Twas like an Eagle in the Sky,
And when the Sky began to lower
'Twas like a Liar at my Door,
When my Door began to crack
'Twas like a Stick across my Back,
And when my Back began to smart
'Twas like an Arrow in my Heart,
And when my Back began to bleed
I was like the Man of Double Deed
Who sowed his Garden full of Seed.

Traditional
Seething. Norfolk

CONTENTS

IN WHICH THE AUTHOR TELLS OF

BALLADS, SONGS, AND RHYMES

ILLUSTRATIONS

CHAPTER 1

CHILDREN'S RHYMES

Plow Monday, Jan. 7th

Tinka-boy, plough boy,
Only once a year!
Gi's tuppence-ha'penny to buy a pint of beer!
If not tuppence-ha'penny a penny will do!
If not a penny still God bless you.

Valentine's Day, Feb. 14th

Good morrow, Valentine,
How it do hail;
When my father's pig die
You shall have the tail.

Good morrow, Valentine,
How it be hot;
When my father's pig die
You shall have the lot.

Traditional: North Norfolk

The Queen's Birthday, May 24th

The twenty fourth of May
The Queen's Birthday,
If you don't give us a holiday
We will all run away.

Harvest

Never stop to prattle
When you hear the wagons rattle
For bright Phœbe is a-rolling to the West.

Traditional

CHAPTER 1

I yet but young, no speech of tongue,
Nor tears withall, that often fall,
From Mother's eyes when child outcries,
Could pity make good Father take.

TUSSER, 1557

I WAS Born in a small villige in Historick Norfolk, seventy and five years Ago. The third Largest County in England, famed for its corn growen lands, beside bein the home of some of the highest Nobility in the Land, and his Majesty the King and Royal Family. It can bost of some fine town shipps, and many Ancient Abbies and Castles and other land Marks. Abler pens than mine have extolled the County of Norfolk, but like many Norfolk men I some times think there is no place like it.

I was Born of Honest Parents that wold have scorned to do any thing to ofend the Laws of the Land. I was an onley Child, and the Brought me up to honer and obey the King and all put in Orthority under him. To keep all the Laws of the Land in Riverence, but I supose there was some latent sporting blood in me, which counted for what I was and what hapened to me after. My Father was a verry religous man, and a Church-man at that; he made me go with him to Church at least twice on the Sabboth day, it was not much wonder if I kicked over the traces wen I got older. I had religon drilled into me, morning noon and night.

He was so honest was my Father, and I grant that he thought what the Parson and his Master said was always right. Perhaps they were, perhaps they were not, but not bein made beliven, as I got older I did not think as he thought—even if I dare not tell him so, I thought so. He was so honest that

3

in these days he could not have lived at all. He was a man those above him could lead any were, and he wold never have questioned there Judgement.

My Mother, God bless her, was quite the reverse of that, but my Father he ruled her and me with a rod of iron in the guse of his religon. He worked forty year on one farm as a Labourer, and never got any higher. No doubt he was a good man, but good as he was wen he could work no more he was not wanted any more. There was no old Age Pension then, so the Parish I think alowed him 2/6 a week, and poor Mother had to go to work in the fields. Did the Parson help them—no he told them to be contented with there lot, and make the most of what they had got.

For many a year after I was grown up my Father never spoke to me nor owned me, I haven gone my own way and taken to ways he had no liken to, but at last he found he had a son, as later on in his old age I helped him and Mother all I could. But he never seam to aprecate my help like poor old Mother did. I think that the old Dad gave up work wen he was sixty five and lived till he was eighty three, so by all his honesty and hard work he died a Pauper, and was Buried in a Pauper grave. He was honest true, but it never made any diffrence to him, in this World anyways.

Not so with poor old Mother as I buried her myself, and kept her for some years, or helped to keep her. She died at the age of Ninety seven and brought my son up, the one that lay out in France, that was the son of my first Wife. She was a Mother to him from the time he was born, he having lost his own, and it was right I should help the Old Lady as far as was in my Power.

Well I think I have told enough of my Parents who have been gone many a year. I know I was a trubble to them, and caused a lot of pain to them both, and how that come about I shall try and tell.

I used to spend a lot of time with my Grandparents on my Mother's side. They were a dear old cupple, and I was verry fond of them and they of me, and would never hear any thing rong of me. I think that in there younger days they had been a bit of a merry lot, and the old man used to sit and tell me of the things that he had done wen he was a young man,

A lot used to go on pack ponies down the green roads.

and I used to sit and listen by the hour. I never herd any thing like that at home from my Father, even if he knew any thing. He would never tell me a tale except about religon, I got plenty of that—much good it done.

He told me tales of the fights he had had with Keepers at nights; tales of the Smuglars that worked all along that coast, and how they used to come up the river and hide there cargoes in holes in the ground. My old Grandad used to tell me a lot about them, he seam to know all there tricks. He never said as much but I beleve he had a dealing with them. Any how he had a pair of old flint Pistolls, and he told me that they were a smuglar's once upon a time.

They used to bring there Boats as far as Lynn wash. The Cargoes came from Holland and Amsterdam, and other parts of Germany, and were Brandy and other Spirits, silks, and many other goods. The Smuglars used to meet what they called Luggers out on Lynn wash, then bring in the cargos and row them up the Nar or take them over land. Of cors that was befor Lynn was a sea port like to day. There were Coast guards in them days and many a fight the smuglars had with them.

There was a lot of oncultivated land called cars and fens and the Smuglars had roads and hide outs in those wildernesses. They used to unload on Terington marshes, and to this day they come across the Smuglars holes that had been timbered up on Marham Fen. Many years ago they used it for turf cutten, so they stored the stuff there till they could get it away. A lot used to go on pack ponies down the green Roads that run all over Norfolk, away from the highways.

Near were Grandad lived there was a verry old Roadside house, and the Smuglars met there at nights to discus there plans. It was down long befor my time and a Farm house built on the site, now called Crossgate

Farm. It is about two hundred yards from the Ancient market Cross wich stand there to day, and a mile from Pentney Abby.

He told me a lot more than I can rember now, it being more than sixty year ago by a good bit. I was never so happy as wen I was listening to his tales of Smugling and other Outlaw tricks, it used to warm my hart to hear them. Wen my Father got to hear that he was tellen me those tales he forbid me goen to see the Old People, but I always managed to get to them some way or another.

He used to tell me about one of there tricks wen they were young, and how they used to get two pigs for one. There was a Squire at West Acre Hall near Swaffham by the name of Antony Hamond, who used to farm the whole of that villige. The Labours would go to the Stewerd and buy a pig, and mark it to take away at the first opitunity. Then they would pick there time and if no one saw them, they would go and take one pig, and then go back again for the one that they had bought. If any one saw them with the first pig they said 'This is the one we bought off the Stewerd', hoping they would get away with it.

My old Granny was a bit of a quack Doctor, and the People used to come to her with all there ills. She was a mid Wife beside, and one to help with the layen out of Boddies. She told me all the Charms and such like that I know, and lernt me lots of old songs and sayens that was goen about in them days, I suppose that some of them was two hundred years old. I can rember some of them but I have never seen them riten down.

I saw in a paper some were about a Doctor sayen it was rong for people to 'draw the pillow' [1] as they do in these parts and nothing but a way of pushen some one off quick. In my Grandmother's time it was the reglar thing to draw the pillow from under the heads of People wen dyen; it was supposed that the last breath left the boddy easier, beside wich the

---

[1] The custom still practised in some Norfolk villages of taking the pillow from under the head of a dying person so that the head falls back and death (especially in the case of old people) is hastened. A doctor unused to local customs started some correspondence on the subject. It arose from the fear there might be doves' feathers in the pillow. The dove is sacred to the Holy Ghost, and those that cling to the Holy Ghost cannot die.—L. R. H.

Boddy became more rigid quicker, and ready for the last Office of layen out. My old Granma used to follow that as well as other things. The bees was always told if any one of the families died, and crape put on the hives, if this was not done they said the bees fretted to death. They had a plan to of ringing in the flights of bees wen they swarmed, by beating cans and such like, but it was not to attract the bees as some thought, but to shew who they belonged to.

The old Lady used to pretend to tell fortunes from the tea cups. Many a time wen I was at hers I used to take the spoon and pull the tea leaves up the Cup, and ask her what she could see for me. She always had some thing. Some times I was goen on a long Jurney, some times I was goen to get into trubble, and that mostly came true, as I was more often in trubble than out of it. They were a queer old Cupple, I think the old Man was ninety wen he died.

Then I used to hear a lot about the horrors of tranceportation. I often think that the old People of the Eighteen Centuary, used the tales of tranceportation as a Bogey man to frighten there sons. The young genera-tionn now would not even know what it means to be tranceported.

I had an Uncle tranceported some where round about that time for Sheep Stealing, and Grandfather have told me many a time about it. He was a Shepperd and lived at West Acre. It was the time that Amerricca was asken for Emergrants to go out, and he stole the sheep to get the money to go there. They told me that he got twenty years sentence, and was sent as a convict to Australia, but wen he got there and it came to serving it he had only to work a few years for the Government, and then he was free to work were he liked, as long as he did not leave the Cuntry.

By there acount he carried on his trade of Shepperd, saved money, married and settled, and wen he died it seam he owned eleven miles square of land, and forty thousand sheep, so it seams there was a good side to that game.[1]

[1] Transportation was looked upon as a dreadful fate. The results were as a matter of fact often most fortunate for the offenders, as in this case. Possibly the length of time it took for communica-

I know he used to send the old People money some times, and they seamed to do fairly well, for my Grandfather did not do any work that I can rember, except he would go mole catchen and rat Poisning on ocasions, wen it suted him. Of corse he was a verry old man wen he told me these tales, he have been dead this fifty year and more, both of them haven lived to a ripe old age. Nothing suted me like goen to listen to him. He and Grandmother were nice old people in my eyes, and I am not shure I did not inherit some of my sporting ways from him.

They used to warn me about the Publick kitchen and say it was the place were all the bad deeds were hatched. I do not beleve that—it would not be the place for secret planing, neither do I belive that many of the bad Jobs that they did in those days were caused by any thing but Povity. Let us rember how much worse the times were than in later years, and they are bad enough now. I think most if not all the trubble was caused by starvation, and hunger will make men do crimes they would look twice befor they atempted for any other reason. I dare say some were done for the love of the thing, and some times for revenge on one of there frends that had treated them rough, but that will always hapen.

Of corse I do not rember, I only know what they told me. The laws of the land were much more severe, and I have read that a man was tranceported for life for stealing two ducks. The harts of the People were much more callous than to day—my Grandfather walked from my home to Norwich, a distance of thirty miles to see Bloomfield Rush the Murderer [1]

tions to reach home, or the entire lack of them, had something to do with the horror it inspired. Also most Norfolk villages, especially in the marsh districts, were at that time almost completely isolated, the inhabitants seldom leaving the confines of the Parish, and going 'foreign', except in the case of sea-faring folk, filled them with terror. According to Mark Taylor they used a 'Life Index' in this fashion: 'A bottle of the prisoner's urine was corked securely and hung up in his old home; then any one knew how he was getting on. If the urine got cloudy, he was ill; if it wasted, he was dead and the family put on mourning.'—L. R. H.

[1] The trial of James Blomfield Rush for the particularly brutal double murder of Mr. Isaac Jermy of Stansfield Hall, Nr. Norwich, and his son (and the attempted murder of the son's wife and a maidservant), caused a terrific sensation at Norwich Assizes, March 1849. He was convicted after eight days' trial, during which he conducted his own defence. The following is an extract from the Judge's sentence: 'It appears from letters that you have yourself put in, that to the father

hung on Castle Hill, and there wer   thousands of people there. I think it
was the last time any one were hung in Publick at the Castle. They had
been tryen him for days and days, and the whole County wanted to se the
end of him, and most of them as could do so got there one way and
another, even if they had to walk.

My Grandfather have told me men were so brutilized that if two of
them fell out, they would settle it by standing and kicking each others
legs till one fell down; or they would have there legs tied under a table
and fight over the top till one was done. Thank God those terible times
are over, but I have not the least doubt that some of the Maderstrates
would be just as Vengeful now on the Poacher if the law alowed it.

I am sure that I should have been tranceported long ago if I had lived
in them days, and am glad I did not, not haven much fancy for them
foreign parts.

I had another Uncle as went all through the Crimen war, was in all the
thickest of the fighting, and then was through the Indian Mutiny and
come out at the end with out a scratch. He had six medels and clasps, and
lived till he was over eightey, and then was throwen out of a cart and
Instantly killed, which seamed a strange fate after all his adventures.

Of my Father's parents I did not know much as they lived many miles
away at a villige called Rougham, and I hardly ever saw them. If they
were any thing like my Father I did not lose much I'm thinking. That is
about all I can rember about them as went before me, it seam as if they
were a bit of a mixture same as most folk.

of the unfortunate victim of your malice you owed a debt of deep gratitude. You commenced a
system of fraud by endeavouring to cheat your landlord. You followed that up by making that
unfortunate girl whom you seduced the tool whereby you should commit forgery, and having
done that you terminated your guilty career by the murder of the son and grandson of your friend
and benefactor. It unfortunately sometimes happens that great guilt is something, in imagination
at least, too nearly connected with something of heroism to dazzle the mind. Fortunately, in your
case you have made vice as loathsome as it is terrible. . . . I tell you you must quit this world by an
ignominious death, an object of unmitigated abhorrence to every well regulated mind' (*Ipswich
Journal*, Saturday, April 7th, 1849).

CHAPTER 2

DREAMS

A Maid to dream of verdant Groves,
She'll surely have the man she loves;
But if the Groves are nipt with Frost,
She'll be as sure in Marriage crost.
A Peacock tells t'will be her lot
To have a fine Man but a Cot.
To dream of Lambs or Sheep astray,
Her Sweet-heart soon will run away.
To dream of letters far or near,
She soon will from her Sweet-heart hear.
To dream of bad Fruit, her Sweet-heart
A fair Face has but false at Heart.
To dream her Sweet-hearts at Church zealous,
If she has him he will be Jealous.
A Maid to dream of Cats, by Strife,
She'll lead but an unhappy Life.
To dream her Sweet-heart will not treat her,
Tis well, if she have him, he dont beat Her.
To dream her Sweet-heart gives a Kiss,
Instead of Blows, she will have Bliss.
If she dreams of Bees or Honey,
When Wife he'll let her keep her Money
And be the Mistress of his Riches,
Nay if she will, may wear the Breeches;
And some times Life is not the worse,
Where GREY MARE is the BETTER HORSE,
To keep things right in stormy Weather,
Thong and Buckle, both together.
To dream of Timber she'll be wed
To one who'll be a Log in Bed;
But she'll be Wed who dreams of Flies,
To one that will be Otherwise.

The New Book of Knowledge, 1758

CHAPTER 2

Peters Brother where lyest all night?
There as Chryst y yod.
What hast thou in thy honde? heauen keyes.
What hast thou in thy tother? Broade booke leaues.
Open heauen gates, Shutt hell yeates.
Euerie childe creepe christ ouer
White Benedictus be in this howse,
Euerye night, Within and without.
                    The Spell of St. Edmund's Bury, 1502

As I have said my old Grandmother taught me quite a bit in the way of charms and doctering, a lot I have forgot, but some I can rember even now, as is the way with what one lerns wen one is young. Not that I held much by Witchcraft and charms and all that the old Lady belived in, although I have come across some of the present day generation that do. Still the world is wiser than what it was in the olden time, but I think weaker.

There was one charm she told me of wich was practiced wen any one wanted to get comand over there fellow Creaturs. Those that wished to cast the spell must serch until they found a walking toad. It was a toad with a yellow ring round its neck, I have never seen one of them but I have been told they can be found in some parts of the Cuntry. Wen they had found the toad they must put it in a perforated box, and bury it in a Black Ant's nest. Wen the Ants have eaten all the flesh away from the bones it must be taken up, and the person casting the spell must carry the bones to the edge of a running stream the midnight of Saint Marks

Night,[1] and throw them in the water. All will sink but one single bone and that one will swim up stream. When they have taken out the bone the Devell would give them power of Witch craft, and they could use that Power over both Man and Animiles.[2]

I rember haven been told of a man and his Team of horses wich had the spell cast on them, and the horses were stopped on the road and would not move backwards or forwards, till the horse man was told to whip his weels, and that took the Power of the Witch away and the horses could move on. Of corse I am not tryen to say that that was true, but it was told to me for truth.

The charm that the old People used to counteract the Power of the Witch was this. Wen they emadgined that they were in Evill hands they must serch and find a fungis that grow from the Witch Elm tree. It is a verry big fungis, the shape and size of a large plate, no doubt every one have seen it, the old People always called it the Devell's tunge. Wen they had got the fungis they must next find the leaves of the Adder's tunge, that herb which is found beside mirie places with leaves shaped some thing like a spear. To this must be added the castor from the inside of a horses fore leg, and some of the blood of the affected one, and some horse shoe nails. The mixture must then be placed in a stone Jug, and the jug put in a fire made with thorn Butts, or in other words the wood of the Thorn tree. Wen the concotion was all Burnt away, the Power of the Witch was dead, but while they were doin it the operaturs had to sit quite still till the Witch was drawn to the doors of the house, and never speak a word, or the charm was useless.[3]

Of corse we know that a great many Women were Burnt and killed

---

[1] April 25th.

[2] 'Another form of this spell is to take toads and put them up the chimney, and as the animals waste in the heat of the fire so the victims of the witch's spite consume away. If the toads shriek it is a sign that the spell has been laid on the person, but if they burst and fall down the spell is removed.'—Mark Taylor, 'Norfolk Folk Lore'.

[3] This was practised in various forms, it being usual to stop up all cracks in the room and make the fire very hot, the idea being that the more the temperature in the room rose the more strongly the witch was drawn towards her victim. If horses or cattle were overlooked, their blood was

for the crime of Witch craft in the old days, and I have set and herd those stories till my blood run cold, but as I got older I did not beleve those tales any more. In some parts you could not make the old People beleve any diffrent but that there was still Witch craft goen on.

The younger Generation do not beleve a lot that the old ones tell them these days. There used to be all sorts of legends in those days, gosts of all sorts, tales of Weanling Calves and shaggy Dogs that walked on the high way, and men riden about with no Heads on, and Panthom Carrages runing about the Cuntry side, I never se none of them but the old People beleved that it was all true.

There was a lot more sense in some of my old Grandmother's cures, but of corse people dont hold by them in the same way as they did now they have lerned the ways of the World and got more Education. There were all sorts of charms for diffrent Ailments. There was one if a child was Born with a rupture. The Father wold go out and serch about till he found a strait young ash plant, wich he could put his knife through and split down. Then they wold bring the Child and holding the ash sapling apart, draw the child through the split. The split parts were pulled together again and bound with string, and as the sapling grew together so the Child's rupture healed. I have seen several of these plants near the old People's houses but I canot say if the charm came true.

Then there was a charm for any one trubbled with bleeding from the nose. They should get a skein of silk, and get nine Maids each to tie a knot in the skein, and then the sufferer must wear it round his neck. That was a shure cure for Nose bleed. The cure for Head acke was to get the skin of the Viper and sew it in to the lining of the hat . . . people would hunt many miles for these skins in the month of April wen the Vipers shot

placed on the fire, and as it boiled the witch was supposed to writhe in agony, which proved her guilt. For the bewitchment of lice, which was well known even in my own time in Norfolk, the cure of a Yarmouth row witch is quoted.—L. R. H.

'She advised the sufferer to cut his finger and toe nails, also his axillary hair, put these in a pan with some of his urine, and stew at midnight. This would force the culprit to appear. If the witch's knock at the door was not answered in a few minutes, the guilty one would burst.'—Mark Taylor.

there skin, and any one finding one could make a good price of it for that purpose.

The villige were I was born was a verry ancient villige and wen I was a boy there were a lot of old houses in it. I can well rember wen every cottage had a horse shoe nailed on the door, and a stone with a hole through it. That was to bring them luck, and preevent Witches from hurting them. In a lot of the old houses in them days you would se the blade of a knife driven in the door posts or the lintle of the door—they used to say that kept the Witches away, but it was all moonshine, I have often cast my memry back and thought how foolish they were.

My Grandmother had a cure of sorts for evrything, and herbs for evry complaint. The Misseltoe was a shure cure for the Hoping [whooping] Cought.[1] Secenction was a good thing for boils, Celendine for weak eys, and Plantain[2] for Limbago, all could be cured some way or another except the rhumatics, and I think that is uncurable.

[1] The most common cure to the present time is a mouse cooked in some form, generally fried. The local Doctor when he first came to South Norfolk was completely at sea when informed that a small patient continued to whoop with unabated vigour in spite of the fact that he had 'had his mouse and all'.

Two other well-known cures are to push the child nine times under a bramble sucker which is rooted in the ground, and to hold a frog in the child's mouth, and then let it loose, when it is supposed to carry away the disease.

[2] The Plantain is famous for its curative properties, and has been from very early times. An old herbal describes it as 'one of those common plants which have so much virtue that nature seems to have made them common for universal benefit'. The following Anglo-Saxon poem on this plant, then called the Waybroad, is found in the Harleian MS. 585.

> 'And thou, Waybroad,
> Mother of Worts,
> Open from Eastward,
> Mighty within;
> Over thee carts creaked,
> Over thee Queens rode,
> Over thee brides bridalled,
> Over thee bulls breathed,
> All these thou withstoodest,
> Venom and vile things
> And all the loathly ones,
> That through the land rove.'—L. R. H.

The olden time People used a lot of Charms for rhumatics, and they do still in many parts. One would carry the bone of the Pig's foot in there pockets, it was the Bone that Joined the foot to the ankle of the pig. Another would carry the first new Potato, the size of a small egg in his, and another a pice of stone sulphur. A verry favrite cure was a pice of brass, a pice of Zince and a pice of Copper in a bag, wich must be worn on the sufferer. Some would put new flanel next the skin and wear it till it would hold on no more.

My old Grandmother always held by the cure of the Dead Hand if any one had what she used to call a Bleeden tumer. Those that were aflicted in this way must find a corpse and place the hand of the dead person upon the part afected by the tumer, and then as the hand of the corpse decaid away, so would the tumer be consumed.[1]

There was a cure for wharts that was some thing of the same idea, there is a certain snail, hod-ma-dod or Dodman as they call them in these parts, that is speckled, and that must be rubbed on the wharts and then stuck on a White thorn bush and as the snail wasted so did the wharts, but I used a diffrent cure to that wich I have done hundreds of times and is verry sucessful.[2] The Leach was greatly used in them days too, for a lot of complaints, arresepliss, and those sort of things, and severe bruses. They were a kind of water snail, verry pretty collierd, and the old Lady used to keep them in glass Jars. They were put on the places and sucked the bad blood away till they were full, and then they wuld cover them with salt and the leach threw the blood up again.

Then there were all sorts of queer legands wich evry child was told. Wen a dog howled it was shure sign of death, or some disaster to come to those that herd it. If a farm yard Hen got the notion of crowen, she had to be killed at once, as that was the onley way to avert

---

[1] Usually the corpse was supposed to be of the opposite sex to the patient employing the cure, and originally seems to have only been considered effective if the corpse was of a person who had been hanged or anyhow died by violence. In the days when every common had its gibbet and suicides were buried at cross-roads this would not have been difficult to accomplish. The cure was also used for 'swelled throat' or goitre.—L. R. H.   [2] See pp. 166–7.

trubble. Her head must then be cut off, and that was suposed to remove the curse.

If a bird flew into a house and flew round three times, that denoted great trubble for the inmates, but if it flew out again at once that was luck for some one. If a large Humble bee flew in the door that was a Stranger comen, and if a Toad come onto the Threshold, and walked away agin, some one was goen a long Jurney, but if it come in and sit down that ment that an Enemy was tryen to hurt one of the household.

There was a lot more of them tales that I have forgot, as its sixty years and more since I have herd them and that is a long time to rember all I have herd.

Then there was a lot of charms the farmers used to beleve in for the Animiles. Wen Cows calved, the after berth had to be hung on a White thorn bush, as it was said to prevent Milk fever and other ills.[1] Do not think that we used to hear so much of that kind of thing as at the present day. No doubt the feeding of cows on artifichell food is responcible for some of it, as I beleve most of the trubble is over flush of milk that force the blood to the cow's brain, as I have seen them die nearly mad. The Old People beleved in there charms but the Vetinary of to day have put all those things away. Of corse there were milk feaver then as well as Foot and mouth disease, but wen the Farmer got that in his yards they did not kill all there beasts but dress them with Stockhollam tar, and salt. I can Just rember wen there was a Cattle Plauge in Norfolk in 1864 and 5, and there was hundreds of Cattle slawtered and burried but not for foot and mouth disease. I rember my Grandfather carrien me with him to kill a lot of Bullocks. He killed scores at diffrent farms.[2]

[1] A stone with a hole in it wrapped up in paper and put on a rafter in the cow-house roof is used in South Norfolk.

When a herd of cows is affected with contagious abortion, the aborted calf should be buried beneath the doorstep so that all the cows will walk over it. The disease is supposed to disappear when the carcase of the calf has rotted away. (I wonder if this custom was inspired by the line in the Litany: 'and finally to beat down Satan under our feet').—From Local Veterinary Surgeon.

[2] This was the Rinderpest—a severe outbreak took place in this year, introduced by a cargo of cattle from Revel.

They would pull up at the word of command.

I do not think they will ever stamp that out—it will alway shew itself in diffrent parts of the Cuntry. I have not the least doubt but what it is carried from the earth to the Cattle, Just as foot rot in sheep, it is much the same thing, but of corse Foot and Mouth can be cured as almost any complaint can be cured except rhumatics.

Another charm the farmers had in them days was if a labourer got a pig he would cut a small pice off the pig's ear, and a small pice off its tail, get some horse shoe nails and put them together in a small bottle, and put it in the fire and let it melt or burst. That was to be shure that the pig would take no harm and do well, and that mattered a lot to a poor man in them days, as they would put all their savings into a pig.

Evry one know that maids look for four leaf clover to bring them fortune—they used to say they onley grow where a mare have dropped her first foal.

Many years ago the horse men in Norfolk had a supernatall Comand over their horses. I have seen one put the Bridles of his horses on there necks and come into the yard at a gallop and they wold pull up at the word of comand. He for one was put down as haven some onnaturell Power, but there were many men that had the same controll over horses in them days. No doubt it was Pacence and a lot of trubble—I was goen to say Crulty but I will not say that, as I have trained a lot of breeds of dogs and I have always found that Kindness have been much better than the wipp.[1]

There was one charm that old Granny used to try and tell me about—the way to find out if a lover cared any thing about you. You must take the Door key and put it between the leaves of the Book of Ruth in the Bible, two people balancen the key by the bow on the midle finger of there hands. The one that wished to know

---

[1] 'A Norfolk "wise woman" who was supposed to have this power made a living by gathering and selling "muck". One day she thought that a farmer who had bought a load was piling up his cart too high, so she cast a spell on his horses so they could not move a step. When he had unloaded the cart to the level she thought right she said "G'won" and they went.'—Mark Taylor's 'Norfolk Folk Lore'.

if the lover was true holden the key on the finger of there right hand as the artist has drawn.

Then these words must be repeated:

'Many Waters canot quence true love, neither can the floods drown it. Love is as strong as Death, but Jelousy is as crucle as the Grave, and burneth with a most vehiment flame. If a man should give all the substince of his house for love, it would be utterly consumed.'

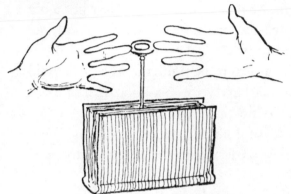

If the book turn to the left the lover will be false and ficcle, but if to the right the lover will be true. The old Lady could nether read nor rite but had a wunderful memery for that sort of thing.

She used to say that the bewitchment of lice was caused by the evell eye of some enimie, and the surest cure for that was to stick a needle through some of the lice, and pin it to the higest boark [baulk, *i.e.* beam] in the house, and that would break the spell. No one perhaps beleve it now, but you must rember that in them days houses were not so much sanitory, and there was more dirt to breed them. To day if a child should happen to have Vermin in there heads at School they are sent home to be cleaned, and the parents sumoned for necklect, and verry proper to, as sience have found a cure for all that. Children were herded like pigs in a sty then, the thicker they slept the warmer they were, and that was a lot of the trubble with vermin, and not the evell eye.

The Old People worked verry much by the moon in there day. They would plant there seeds and set there fowles by the Moon. Wen it was risen and in the second quarter they said that the seeds Germated better and quicker, and eggs set then were shure not to go bad under the hens.[1] They

[1] Local farmers still will not allow the veterinary surgeon to 'cut' (castrate) calves or pigs except at the time the new moon is waxing. Those who believe this are said 'To follow the moon'.— L. R. H.

took a lot of notice of the signs of rain, there is many a thing in the cuntry side will tell you that, but some of them one does not hear these days.

If they saw a frog with a bright yellow skin that was a sign of a dry time, but if black in the skin they were shure for rain sone. The same if the cat washed over its ear.

As to the moon ruling the seeds, I do not know if there is any thing in that, but I know that it rule wild Animiles, such as rats and Rabbitts, and all Animiles that are born blind. You will find that they travell much further wen the moon is on the rise than wen it is on the waste. Rabbitts will trap and snare a lot further from there burries, and rats will eat poison more readly than at the fall of the moon. I have been an expert on that sort of thing all my life long, and have proved it many and many a time. Moles will throw up more hills the first two quaters of the moon than the last two quaters, as any one can see if they trubble to take notice.

They used to be a lot of ague in them days in the Marsh lands, Marsh fever as they used to call it [1] but I have not herd of a case for many a year, except in men comen home from India or some such part. The cure was hot beer with mustard seed boiled in it, wich was counted a fine powerful remedy, as were the seeds to bring back speech in palsy.[2]

There used to be a spring of water at a place called Marham, called Maid's Hole, and they said wen I was a boy that to drink from that spring was a cure for the ague. But as I said its gone from the marshes it seam, like the Jack o' Lantern they used to talk about. I have seen some thing like that on the Marsh, flyen up and down, but I used to think it was some insect wich was eluminated. I never could get near one, I have tried some times, but they apear and disapear verry quickley.

I think I have told most of what I herd and lernt from my Grandparents of the old People a hundred years ago. Some of them that practiced those ways would have been a lot more than that had they lived till now. I have come acros some of the present Generation that beleve some of it still as

[1] Malaria—vanished since the marshes were drained.
[2] Laid on the tongue.

I have said befor, but the World is wiser than it was. Perhaps I lernt as much from them as I did at school, but then schools was diffrent to as I shall try and tell.

NOTES ON CHAPTER 2

The following charm may be of interest. It was found among the papers of Thomas Colson, a fisherman of St. Clements, Ipswich, who was drowned in October 1811. He had the nickname 'Robinson Crusoe' and a considerable reputation as a wizard. The note below is his own comment and written in his hand-writing.—L. R. H.

A CHARM

to make a young woman seem to be in love with a young man

Take new wax, and the powder of a dead man, make an image with the face downward and in the likeness of the person you wish to have; make it in the ouers of mars and in the new of the mone; under the left arm-poke place a Swaler's hart and a liver under the rite; you must have a new needal and a new thread; the Sprits name must be menchened, his Sine and his Character.

I take this opportunity to inform my frinds that about 16 yeares ago this Charm was put in practice by sum willians of Witches at Needham-Markett, William Studd been one of them; and they have put me to much torment and lamed me many times, they own to me that they make use of part of the bones of Mrs Wilkerson of Felixtow, she that suffred at Rushmere sum yeares ago; this is sartainly true, and I am ready to give it on oth if required.—THOS. COLSON.

Acts the 9 and 5: It is hard for thee to kick against the pricks.

Contributed to the *Suffolk Garland* (published in 1818) by Mrs. Cobbold of Holy Wells, Ipswich.

A MODERN LOVE CHARM

The man must take an orange, prick it all over in the pits of the skin with a needle, and sleep with it in his armpit. The next day he must see the woman he loves eat it. I was told this was 'a certain love charm, given reasonable opportunity'.—L. R. H.

CHAPTER 3

THE SMUGGLER'S BOY

One cold blowy morning abroad I did steer
By the wide rolling ocean so blue and so clear;
I heard a poor Creature that in sorrow did weep,
Saying, Alas my poor Father lost in the deep.

Your pity I crave to give me employ,
Or forlorn I must wander, a poor Smuggler's boy;
To Holland we sailed while the thunder did roar—
The storm smote us cruelly, far from the shore.

Masts, sails, and rigging sank into the waves
And found with my Father a watery grave;
I jumped overboard and clasped him to me,
But his cold clay was lifeless, and sank down in the sea.

I clung to a plank and so came to shore;
Bad news for poor Mother—Father no more.
She died broken hearted, nor heeded the moan
Of the poor Smuggler boy left to wander alone.

A Lady of Fortune she heard him complain,
Took him into her house out of the wind and the rain.
She said—Neither Father nor Mother have I,
So will pity the Orphan till the day that I die.

He done his work well and earned a good name.
The Lady did die—he the Master became.
She left him her houses and money and land—
So if you are poor you may live to be grand.

Obtained in MS. from the Author

CHAPTER 3

How through the briers, my youthful years,
Have run their race;
O painfull time for every crime!
What touzed ears, like baited bears!
What bobbed lips, what jerks, what nips!
                                    TUSSER, 1557

My Parents did there best for me, and sent me to school, and there I lerned those things they thought proper, reading, and Aritmatics, the colleck for the week, and Beleff and that sort of thing. Also to Honer and obay the Queen, and order ourselves lowley and revently to ower Pastors and Masters; to keep all the Comandments and walk in the way of the rightus all ower lives. We used to read the Bible one hower in the mornings, and do Aritmatic in the afternoon. The girls had to lern to sew and knit, so you see we were all told those things that we should do, but I am afraid with many of them it was as with me—it was soon forgot, once we had left school.

You will hear many an old man say he went to work at seven year old, and did not know a letter in the book. There was good reason for that. If they had lerned any thing at school they went to work in them days so young that they never practized reading or riting, and so forgot all that they had lerned. Wen they were done with the day they were only too ready to eat there megre tea and get them to bed, haven been on the farm from six in the morning till six at night. There were no limited hours for youngsters then, and men did not favour them, there was the word and the blow—and mostly the blow came first. All the lerning they had got was starved and worked out of them.

The children in the school were made up in classes, as they are these days, first class, second class, and so on, but not many ever reached the first class if it hapened that they come from large families. There was no age limit then for leaven school, a boy or girl could leave any time that they could find a Job of work to go to, and that had to be sone if there were a lot of them, or there was nothing to eat.

Of corse they were not all like that, some would lern more wen they left school than they did wen they were there, them that had a liken for reading and riten, but they were few.

As a school Boy I was as fond of mischeef as any other Boy, I got into many a scrape, and I will tell you how it was that I left school in the end. There were two villiges went to one school, as is often the way in Norfolk even in these days, and of corse as a result we were always fighting each other. The master belonged to the opossing villige, and many a caning did we get from him, wether we had desarved it and been the agressors or no. Some of the older ones, me encluded resolved to mutney if he flogged us any more . . . he did, and so we did.

So one day we turned the Master out of school and locked him out. The School was maniged by two of the Farmers and the Clergyman. They came down and stood outside, and promised to lett us off and forgiv us if we would come out. We would not at first, but of cors we had to come out in the end to go home, and wen we did they began on us and we on them. We had aranged to get out by the back way, so we got to the road befor they knew that we were there. There were plenty of stones in the Road, and we verry sone shewed that we could throw them all rite.

Well the end of that was that they turned about six of the worst of us out of school for good, and forbid us to go there any more, so that was the end of my lerning. A lot we cared as there was plenty of work for Boys in them days.

I can tell you we did some queer pranks, wen my old Grandmother herd of my doins, she used to smile and say 'boys will be boys' but it does seam to me looken back that we were a lot more mischerfull than the lads are now.

There was one thing we did that we thought was rare sport. We would get a ladder and put it up to a low cottage, block up the Chimney and tie up the door, so that no one could get out of it, and so smoke the Folks inside out of there windows. Another trick was to set fire to the Comons and many other games of that sort. If there was a field wich People went across, us Boys would take the gate off the hinges and stand it up so that any one comen along and goen to open it, down it would come, bruisen there legs proply. Or we would dig holes in the garden paths so the People stuck there feet in them and fell down.

Another favrite game was in places were there was a well chain that would reach to the door of the cottage, we boys would snap the chain onto the door handle. Of corse we got caught some times and got a good floggen, but if that did happen we always got our revenge some how.

Some of the boys would get a dog and tie a tin can to its tail and send it down the road, but that was a game that I did not like as I was always verry fond of dogs, but a cat or a squerrel hunt was a verry favrite pastime in my young days. In fact I think that any kind of sport or hunt was my delight. Times are altered now and there are more police to look after the bad Boys, still I some times call to mind a little song wich went about years ago, wich had some truth in it I'm thinken.

Wen I was young
Then boys were boys
And went to bed at ten,
And did not smoke
Them stinking fags
Nor ape the ways of men.

Wen I was a little older the Clergman died, and a much younger man came and took his place. He was quite a different man to the old one, and took a great intrest in the boys and young men in the Parish. He organised a Night School, and games in the long summer evenings, wen there was a lot of time for mischeef.

He sone got to hear that I was a bit onruly, but some how he seamed to take a liken to me, even from the first, and used to come and ask me to go to his classes. I was a bit doubtful of doin that and it was some time befor I would consent to go, and told him I had no fancy to be Preched at, or any thing of that kind, I had enough of that from my Father. But I did go in the end and I do not think he ever gave me a word of that sort, just treated me kindly. True he wold some times talk to me for my good, and some People thought that I was getten better and quieter, but I am sorry to say I was some thing like the Smugglers and the Self rightus People; I was working in the dark as much as possible.

I used to go to Sunday School, and rember verry well bein put up to recite the Legand of the Swaffham Tinker, and can rember most of it to this day. It was at a Sunday School party at Pentney School.

The Legend have been handed down from Father to son by the People of Swaffham for hundreds of years.[1] They say that the Tinker repaired Swaffham Church with the treasure he found, any way his effegy still lay in the Church Isle with his baggs and dog by his side—any one can se it there.

Looking back at them days I am thinking that if I was never verry good I was never verry bad as a boy, at least in my owen site, even if I was a bad case in other People's eyes. As a lad I made up my mind to be an outlaw, and I kept it up all through as much as posible. It was a rough road at times in my life, but I suceeded fairly well. But those days are gone a long way, though as I sit alone by my fire side I often think of them.

I stayed at School till I was thirteen years of age, but duren that time, wen I was a boy about nine year old, some thing hapened. I was with Father in the garden, it was winter time, and snow on the ground. Well

[1] See Chapter 4.

without a thought he shewed me were a hare had been eaten his plants off. I made up my mind wen I saw that that I would get her.

There was a big trap hangen up in the shed, it had hung there as long as I rembered. I got it down wen Father had gone, and sit the trap in the snow. Wen I come home from school the next morning of cors the first place I went to was to look at the trap, and you bet I was something pleased to find the hare there. I verry sone beat the life out of her, and carried it to Mother. She near had a fit at what I had done, and carried it upstairs and put it under the bed.

As sone as Father come home I went to tell him, I had not got far with my tale befor he caught me by the coller and gave me the soundest floggen a boy ever received. He thought to stop me from playen those tricks in the futur, but it seam that the seed was sowen by that hare, and it did not take long to germate.

Not long after I rember well me and another Boy was goen up a hedge and we found some snars. Of cors I had to make shure how they were put, and then we took them up, and not many days after that I tried my hand at that game. I rember well the next morning taken two hars.

The next thing was to know what to do with them. There hapened to be a Chap in the villige that harked fish [a fish hawker], so I spoke to him, and he told me he wold take all I could get, as he went to Market twice a week. I think that he gave me three shillings for them—the most money that I had ever posessed at that time as you may guess. I sone tried again, and as a lad I was verry lucky, as I knew how to keep my owen Counsell, and no one suspected me, and as time went on many a hare found its way into the fisherman's house.

Well the time came for me to find some work. Some readers as rember those days may wonder why I did not go to work in the fields as the children did, and as I shall tell later. The ancer is simple—I had to bad a reputation for them Jobs, they wanted me were they could se me, or thought they could! For my part I always had a horor for that sort of work, although I had many a flogging at that time to make me se diffrent.

Poor old Mother screened me all she could, as most Mother's will. I have often thought in after life of the limb I was and the trubble I gave her, and regreted it, but regrets dont mend no broken crocks. I think I am now payen the price—now that I am left alone to think of the days that are gone, my owen children thousands of miles away from me, one in India, the other in Canada, wich I may never se any more.

The first Job I had was what was called Copper Hole Jack, I had to light the fires, help the servants and make myself generally useful all round. Now a lad like that would be called a House Boy, and verry Properly be put in uniform. The People that I went to work for were Gentleman Farmers, Paul was the name, of Pentney lyen east of Lynn. A straggling villige but bosted a fine old Abbey and an ancient Market Cross.

He was not a bad sort of man as a Master went. He had three daughters, and they were verry kind to me, as they knew what I had been through. I do not mean that they gave me any thing, but they always had a cheery word for me and that made a lot of diffrence. They knew I had been a reglar Church goer, and sang in there quire, and they were verry much intrested in the Church and used to play the Orgun.

They tried to make me think that I was some one after all, even if I had been a bad boy, but they could never persude me to go there any more, as I well knew why I had that Job—so that they could keep there eye on me, and I should not have so much chance to do what I should'nt ought.

I can verry well rember in that first Job, the Policeman would often as not walk out and ask me what I had in my Pocket, and serch me befor all my other mates. You will agree that that was verry humilating to me and the stain of that sort of thing wen one is a lad stick for life. I have had lots of Jobs a long way from my Native home, but the stain of what I did

They put me to sheep feeding.

as a youngster have folowed me there. In these days things is diffrent for
boys as are made wanting a bit of adventure. Then there were hundreds
of old People that were never in all there lives ten mile from home from
there cradle to there grave. They do say that the Norfolk villiges are some
of the most lonly in the cuntry, and for hundreds of years no famlys
married out of there own people.

Some of the young men fifty and sixty year ago even, were contented
enough if they could go to a fair once a year, or Lynn Mart. Never
thought of any thing else but what there bed and there work and there
food could give them. But some were as full of mischeef as they could
be—they had no sports to go to, and nothen to ocupy there minds but
what they could find for themselves in the spare time they had. Do not
think I am a lerned scholer, but all my life I have been a keen observar of
men and there habbitts, and it is a true sayen that the Devell always find
some thing for idle hands to do.

Now all that is changed as evry one know. Bicicles have made it posible
for evry one to get about and go fifty mile from home if they chose. So it
has come about that the young Generation both males and females have
lerned the ways of the world. We se plain proof of that evry day. They
run the streets at night and get in all sorts of compney, and not good
Compney mostly. Then there is the Cinemars and Dance halls, they
are all Hells kitchen and another great hindrence to the young and
enexperenced mind. I am not condeming those places of entertainement,
but some of them places are to tempting for the Young people, they
are not the places morality to find, as I have noticed myself. Still
some boys is made they must go over the traces some way, and girls
the same.

I had to be at work at 6 A.M. till 6 P.M. and Sundays much the same
owers. In these days boys want to get to work at 8 A.M. and have a half
day off some times—there was no hollidays in them days. As you can
Judge bein as I was I did not like that Job much, and looked about for a
change.

After a littel I got a Job as Page boy to a Shepperd. It was more to my liken there—I could carry on the game to my hart's content. Of corse the Shepperd was as bad as I was, no one ever gussed our Job, and the frend I have spoken of was the ritcher by many a hare, so were our pockets after a time.

I got too big for sheep keepen, so winter time comen they put me to feeden sheep, cutten turnips and such like. That job I did not mind, although I had to put up with a lot of Wet and Cold.

Not far from were I was there was a big wood called Narbrough Contract, and there a lot of Phesants used to come out and feed. Well I got the Idia I could snare them, and I sone rigged some snars and had a try. I was not verry sucsesful at first, but sone got the hang of that Job, and will tell later on how it is done. I rember I used to get as many as ten in one day. Well I was never suspected and got on fairly well, but sheep feeden like evry thing else come to a finish, and haven time on my hands I must needs go and get had, and not over Phesants ether.

It was this way. In the villige there was a large amount of Comon land, of corse it was enclosed as there were plenty of rabbitts there, and I sone got to work snaren them. Some kind frend gave me away and wen I went one morning there was a Police man and a Keeper there waiten for me. They did give me a chance of getten away with [getting rid of] the rabbitts in my hands, but they swore I had some in a bag. As a matter of fact I never saw any in the bag till they shewed me some.

Well of corse they sumoned me, and to make the case as bad as they could they told a lot of lies as well. Wen it came to it the Justice of the Piece sentenced me to a Months hard Labour, wich I did at Norwich Castle.

In those days if a lad did a bit rong it was Prison for him, now he is given a chance as a first ofender. I am thinking that if I had been treated with a bit of leancy in my first ofence, and been spoken a bit kindley, I might have pulled up, and not have been so bitter as I was.

Dear Reader, it was hard lines to send a Boy to Prison for killing a rabbitt. No doubt that the Maderstrates thought to cure me with a lesson, specially as the Police had painted me so black to them. In these days they try to make a first ofender se the rong of his ways by treating him kindley, much the best plan as I beleve a boy can be led by kindness much better than by the harsh manner they treated them fifty or sixty years ago.

Be that as it may I know that they soured me to the Laws of the Land by that treatment, though there is no telling if any man would go a diffrent way to what he has in the end. I always was a belever in Fate.

CHAPTER 4

THE LEGEND OF THE SWAFFHAM TINKER

John Chapman was a Tinker who lived in Swaffham Town,
One night he dreamed a voice did say if he would win renown,
Then he must go to London Bridge, and there the voice did cry
He'd find a man to tell him where wondrous treasure lies.

So Chapman came to London Bridge, but no man did he see,
Till a Butcher's boy came whistling by, so careless and so free;
As he passed he did let fall a sheep's head on the ground,
And Chapman said to a passer by, 'Oh see what I have found'.

The man he said that all was well, the sheep's head he'd restore,
But first good friend as you seem tired pray tell me now some more.
What brought you up to London to seek this City wide?
Said John, 'A dream brought me to London—a fool's game I have tried'.

'Yes, friend, you are most foolish, to leave your home like this,
To wander up to London, for dreams of fancied bliss,
Where no man care for others, save as they serve their plan,
To rob and slay each other, and best their fellow man.

'Now hark to me a month ago, while sleeping in my chair,
I thought I heard some Church bells chiming clearly in the air,
Then voices hovered o'er me, that seemed to me to say,
Neath the Eastern door of Swaffham Church great treasure buried lay

'I dreamed that I had found a coffer of many guineas bright,
Then I searched again some thirty rods, till there came into sight
A heavy moss grown arch of stone, and after that a cross,
Then I deeper dug for others that lay like useless dross.'

36

He who jested did not notice the change in Chapman's eye,
Nor heeded he the tremor, his dog Jaspar did descry.
Through common, lane, and byway, homeward he quickly sped,
When money failed he tinkered to earn his daily bread.

A comely Widow where he halted offered heart, and house, and barn,
And you who smile and read this, therein can see no harm,
But Chapman never tarried, his heart was not his own,
He knew his wife and children waited for him at home.

At length he reached his cottage door to hear his good wife's cry,
'God bring me back my husband to bless me er'e I die'.
But still he never lingered save to light his lantern at the fire,
And hurried through the churchyard till at last he reached the spire.

There was the Arch stone surely, and lifting proved the key,
For below he found the shining gold of wonderous mystery.
He filled his leather apron quite full ten times or more,
And then with superhuman strength the coffer home he bore.

He cleaned it bright and shining, and on the coming day
There passed two men of learning, 'Why look you here', said they.
'Of what is this inscription—"Beneath me you will find,
Another one containing much treasure of the same kind."

'This is an ancient coffer from Norman times methinks,
The Tinker sees no value, save to buy him meat and drink.'
Now all who read this legend let it be true or not,
Can learn a weighty lesson that must not be forgot.

Obtained in MS. from the Author

Tradition says that John Chapman built the North Aisle of Swaffham Church in 1402 with the money that he found. 'With glasyng, stoling, & pathyng of the same wyth marbyll, & did give to makying of the new stepyll in money besyde the premissis cxxli' (Black Book or Terrier of Swaffham Church).—L. R. H.

CHAPTER 4

A Prison is a house of care,
A place where none can thrive,
A touchstone true to try a friend,
A grave for men alive.
Sometimes a place of right,
Sometimes a place of wrong,
Sometimes a place of rogues and thieves,
With honest men among.

Inscription on the Old Prison, Edinburgh

PRISON life as it was nearly seventy years ago is pretty well stamped upon my memry. To begin with I was convicted at Grimstone in Norfolk, and as I have said befor I was scarce more than a child wen it hapened. But then Maderstrates were much more severe in them days with young ofenders, than they are to day specially wen the charge was Poaching.

I was taken to Norwich by train, handecuffed to a Police man. Wen I got to Norwich I was led along through the streets the same way like a real dangerous fellow. There were no Cabs then for prisners, and evry one could have a good stare at me as I went by. No doubt some people said 'He have done some thing bad' and some may have said, 'Poor kid'— be that as it may I know it seamed a long road to me through the streets, but a last we arived at the Castle Entrance. A door swong open and a Turnkey led us inside. I shall never forget what I felt when I first saw that gloomy Place, and I was just fit to cry, but held back my tears some how.

Well the Turnkey told me to turn out my Pockets wich I did. There was not much in them, but I rember in one was a little cake my Mother had put in there for me, he wanted to know why I had not eaten it befor, but I was to frightened to answer him. The next thing I had to do was to strip off my clothes, and be looked over to se if I had any marks or scars on my boddy. Then they rote down the colour of my eyes and hair, and weight and age.

Wen I was done with all that I was pushed out into a cold passage naket as I was Born, to wait till the Bath was ready. I had to go through with that, and then he brought me shirt and socks, and a sute of clothes covered all over with the broad Arrow, and a number to wear on my Jacket. I forget now what it was, but I used to know well enough.

Then I was put in my cell. The Cell was about ten feet long by six broad, and had a stone floor, and a board for a bed wich the Turnkey shewed me how to put down and make. He brought me a loaf of bread about the size of a good Apple and a can of water, and told me that that was my tea. The bread was brown and hard, made up of maze meal and wheat meal mixed, but it did not matter to me what it was like—I did not want a bite that night as I was fairly done. I kept on thinken of Mother and home, and the trubble I had been and got myself into, just like some had always said I would, and yet tryen all the time to keep up my spirits. I was glad wen the Turnkey told me to undress and to put my cloes outside and then to get to bed.

I will try and tell what it was like as it was a queer sort of bed. There was the bed bord with a raised wooden pillow, but no matress for the bord. For the rest of the things in the cell there was a stool to sit on, and a small table built in the wall to get your meals on. There was a wash bow and a water Jug, and another utincile. I was given a wooden spoon to ea with, but no knife or fork is wanted there.

You had a Bible and prair Book and a himn book, and some times the Parson would come along and leave some littel track. He would some times come and se you, to tell you the enormity of your crime, and warn you that it wold lead you to even worse things, if you did not behave

better in futur. I used to hate the sight of him, it may have been rong of
me but I felt like that.

Now to tell you what the work was, for they made me tread the weel,
and pick okum, wich was hard old tarry rope, not that that killed me by
a long way, but it was then I made a vow that I wold be as bad as they had
painted me.

You were called up at six in the morning, got dressed, made your bed
up, and with a pail of water had to scrub the floor and table and make
evry thing bright and clean for the day. Breakfast at seven thirty to eight
o'clock, then half an hour in Chappel—and was suprisen to hear how the
Prisners sang the himns. Nine o'clock we were marched off to the Weel
room. There there were numbers posted up from one to twelve. The
Warder in charge would shout out what numbers he wanted to work on
the Weel, and those men wold stamp it round for fifteen minutes and then
come off for five minutes. It was like walking up steps and never geting
any higher, but verry hard work and we was kept at it from nine till
twelve.

Then came diner, wich was one pint and a half of stirabout, composed
of one pint of oatmeal, and half a pint of maze meal put in the oven
and baked. We were put on the Weel again from one o'clock till four
of the afternoon, then we were set to pick okum till eight, wen we went
to bed.

Evry Prisner was suposed to work twelve owers a day. I have seen men
get so done they would fall off the Weel in a faint. Wen this hapened they
were put back in there cell to wait for the Docter next day, and if he said
they were shaming, they were punished by taken some of there marks
away from them, so they were much longer getten on to the next stage.

I had to do two weeks in the first stage, and then I got to the second
stage. Then it was the same rutine of work, the mill and okum picking,
but the food was altered. On Monday it was one onze of cooked beef,
and six onzes of potatoes, and four of Bread. Tuesday, six onzes of Suet
pudding, and six of bread. Wensdays, half an onze of fat Bacon, and four

onzes of Harrocat beans and six of bread. Breckfast remained the same
all the time. Them that had more than one month in Prison got No. 3.
diet, but I did not get to that as my time was expired.

On the whole I was fairly lucky and did not have to hard a time. The
Turnkey Warder was getten old and about to retire, and he pitted me
for my age, and would pass my task if it was not finished, only telling me
to try and pick more next time. I think I was the youngest Prissner there
at that time. I might explain that a Prissner get eight marks a day if he
have done his work well and behaved him self. He also got one penny
for evry twelve marks earned, provided it did not exceed ten shilling. As
I have said the way that a man was punished was by taken some of his
marks away from him.

Refractory prissners were locked in dark Cells, and given bread and
water for as many days as the Governer had given them.

There is a lot of diffrence now in the Prissons. Some kind and Human
Gentleman visseted the Old Castle and said that it was not fit for Human
Beins to be shut up there, so it was Condmed, and a new one built, much
better and the Prissners Rutine made much easier. Prisners now are treated
like human Beins, in the old days they were treated more like Wild
animiles. Of corse there was a lot of diffrence in the Warders. Some were
verry ready to get a man punished, others would over look lots of things.
But they like the Prisners were looked after pretty sharp by the Head
Warders, and others put over them.

Well I finished my month, and as I looked a bit fagged out I was given
a small loaf of bread to help me along home with. I did not touch it but
took that loaf home and hung it up in the house wen I got there. It hung
there a long time and some hard memries hung with it.

Wen I got home every one looked at me as if I had done some terrible
crime, or I thought they did posibly. If I had had some one to have shewn
me a little kindness then or pitty, it might have been a turning point in
my life, as I had been through a hard time for a lad like me. But there
was none to do that except my old Mother.

I rember well enough the Clergyman meeting me on the road one day, not long after I come home. He stopped me and wanted to know how I liked Prisson. It seamed to me he asked it with a sneer, any how I knew I cut him off pretty quick, and I never entered his Church again.

It is a long time since those days but many is the time I have walked through the Beautifful rooms of Norwich Castle, now that it is a Museum and thought of the weeks I spent there in Prisson, and of all the missery and sufferen that have been endured inside the Walls of that Historick Building.

Of the New Prisson I have nothing to say here, but that I should prefere that to the Poor Law Institution if I had to Choose. The food is more fit for human Beins now, the Cells are comfortable and evry man have a better Chance. By industry and if he want to he may get a good Job. They have five acres of garden, and lots of the men are engaged working in them. The work is much more intresting, and the prisners have conserts evry other Sunday and lectures on week nights, and evry one can atend them. A Prisner have a knife and fork to get his food with, and bread and butter for his breckfast, and tea or a pint of cocoa for each meal.

The Discipline is kept up but in a much more human way. A Prisner may shave twice a week, and is alowed to have his own safety raysor if he have one.

Wen we hear or read in the papers of some one escapen, do not think dear Reader that it is any the better for them that are left, it make the survilence much more acute.

There is one thing that I should like to say to all those who read this book, and that is never you go to Prisson if you can avoid it. It is not the Punishment that hurt you, it is the dark looks and jeers of other People that hurt wen they know that you have been there. Once done it canot be undone, for the Police are ever on your track. Many a man would have pulled up if it had not been for them—they wisper to a Master 'He have been in Prisson' and blite all his good resilutions.

I know well enough, who better, and can prove it, that in a good many cases this taint never leave a man, no matter what his crime have been, or if he is guilty or not.

Well I have told how I came back—it did not seam to have done me much good, and wen things got bad I supose I went much the same way as I had been befor. Any how the time came wen my Parents were forced to turn me out from home, as Father lived on the Farm, a place he had held for forty year for the same farmer as I have said befor, and he could not put up with my ways about the place.

That was the time that I made up my mind I must leve home for good, and I went and hired a small cottage. I was my owen Master then, and so cared not a darn for any of them. It was then that I begun to think I would go a bit farther than I had gone befor, and wen I was at Lynn one day I bought a small 20 bore gun. That was the first gun that ever I had, and buyen it proved the start of a lot that I did in later years.

I rember bein out one morning Just at day break, and I saw some thing comen in the arly morning light, some thing that looked odd to me. I waited till it come up to me, and wen it got there I found it was a fair size pig that had been shacken some were and had strayed. Well a charge of shot between the eys and ear soon put that right. Here again my frend the Fisherman come in to get rid of it. I think he gave me a cupple of pounds for that pig, and I never herd a word more about it.

Well the season come round again, and haven got a gun, for the first time in my life I tried my hand at the Birds on the trees, and found it a most Pleasing Job. First I worked one quater and then another, always shiften about and never goen to a place twice in a week. I have killed as many as I could carry at a time many a night. I rember well the most I ever killed alone was thirty five birds. Some times I was five or six miles from home, so dear Reader you will se that it was hard work carrien them birds so far.

After a time I got to know frends round a bout in the diffrent places that I worked, so I could leave the swag there.

The Fisherman too—he harked his fish in that direction, so he would

bring the birds home for me. The Police tried everything to catch me.
They would come and tie cotten on the handel of the cottage door to see
if I was gone out or not, but I knew that and never went poaching from
my home, but from friends, or else lay out till I could get to work with
my nights dervation.

Just at that time to my shame I got linked with a young woman, but
I must tell how through that I got the best pall I ever had and come to the
happiest time in my life.

CHAPTER 5

A SONG

HE.   If you with me will go, my love,
You shall see a pretty show, my love,
Let Dame say what she will;
If you will have me, my love,
I will have thee, my love,
So let the milk pail stand still.

SHE. Since you have said so, my love,
Longer I will go, my love,
Let Dame say what she will;
If you will have me, my love,
I will have thee, my love,
So let the milk pail stand still.

Traditional: From the *Suffolk Garland*

THE PLOUGHBOY'S SONG

A starry night for a ramble
In the flowery dell,
Through the bush and bramble,
Kiss and never tell.

I like to take my sweetheart out
(Of course you do says she)
And softly whisper in her ear,
'How dearly I love thee'.

When you picture to yourself
A scene of such delight,
Who would not take a ramble
On a starry night.

Traditional: West Norfolk

CHAPTER 5

Behold of truth, with wife in Youth,
For joy at large; what daily charge
Through children's hap, what opened gap,
   To more begun.
The child at nurse to rob the purse,
The same to wed to trouble head;
For pleasure rare, such endless care,
   Hath husband won.

TUSSER, 1557

IT was perhaps a fellow feeling as drew us together in the begining, as she poor girl was as much persequted as I had been. She was a servant up at a Gentleman Farmers not so far away from were I was liven, and of corse she had her night out like other servants. She was just eighteen years old, the same age as myself wen I got to know her and she started bein frendly with me.

As soon as it was known that she and I was palling up, those that she worked with, and others, tried by every means in there power to stop her, thinken no doubt that I was no proper compney for her, she haven no parents, and no one to go to. But it was all to no purpose, she would have her way.

Wen ever I went to meet her I used to take my dogs with me if the night was rite—or my gun. Many and many a night she came out with me, for she was no hindrence to the game. She could run and Jump as well as me and there was few could beat me at running wen I was a Young man. She could carry as many Birds to—and carryen Birds is no light Job. Many a hare have she carried under her coat for me, and many a Phesant. As it was all Cuntry round that part we had some good sport.

Well I supose that tale got about, and wen they found that they could not stop her from me, they gave her notice to leave her place. There was sevrell Ladies round about who was intrested in her, and put themselves about to get her a place in London at good wages so she should be out of my way. But no she stayed, and stuck to me through thick and thin, wich she could do as she had no parents, and no one to controwl her, so she went what way she wanted.

As I have rote befor, I had a home of my owen to take her to, as sone as she was ready to come, and after a bit she did come, and shared it with me for about four years or more.

My Cottage stood back from the main road some thirty or forty yards, with a path running acros the field at the back wich I could use wen I liked, wich come about this way.

We was out one night, me and her, and we came acros two colts stuck in a muddy dyke, properly bogged they were, with only there heads and backs out of the mud. They had got in were the bottom was hard and walked along to were they sunk in.

It was about mid night and I went and called the Farmer up, and told him what had hapened to the colts, and he got up and called some of his men, and they went and got them out. I did not stop to help him, as I did not want his men to know I had been there, but the Farmer was grateful and did not tell on me.

The land runing behind my house belonged to him, and after that we had an arangement, and he gave permision to use that path wen ever I wanted to get home that way, and no questions asked—but of cors that was a secret between him and me.

Just at the back of the Cottage was a round wall called the Old Pound, were years befor they used to put strayen cattle. That was done away with a long time ago, but the pound come in useful as it aforded us good cover to get home many a night wen we had been out on the Job. I do not

They went and got them out.

know wether some spechell Providence watched over us, be that as it may we always got home safe.

After about three years things fell out so that it became Imperitive that we got married. . . . I have no need to tell why. She was one of the best palls that a man ever had, and the best wife any man could want. Do not think dear Reader that I am telling a love story, but it is true that I loved her more than any thing else on this earth and she loved me the same. It was not only me that loved her neither, for it always seam she had a way with her with all live things, and pets and birds.

I rember once bringing home some young hedgehogs as I had meant for the ferrits. Queer pale looken little things they are then with there spines all soft. Well my wife got hold of one of them and brought it up on bread and milk. It got so tame it would come to her wen she called its name, and you could pick it up and handle it same as you could a kitten, for it would lay all its spines down flat, and close to its boddy.

Then she had Jays and Jackdaws I got for her out of the woods, and she would bring them up by hand. The Jay could say any thing and so could the Jackdaw, and I have seen her many a time going out with the birds flying after her and sitting on her shoulder. They would go shopping with her wen she went down the villige street, and sit on the top of the shop till she come out. In fact she seam to be able to fasanate the birds and beasts she took a fancy to—all except cats and them she could not bear.

Many is the happy time she and I had together duren them years, and many a joke to, but come fair come foul she always stood by me. Once she saved my life. I had shot a Phesant on the branch of a tree hangen over the side of a pond wich was frozen up with ice. I reched to get it and the bough I had hold on broke, and I plunged through the ice into the pond, and was nearly smothered in the mud. She got the gun and reached down to me and I got hold of it and some how she pulled me out, but if I had been alone I must have smothered in the mud.

It seam I was never meant to drown as I rember well as a boy diving

in the Nar and striking my head on a root and layen at the botom of the
river onconcious, but they pulled me out in time.

I rember once I and the wife were out netten hars one night and had
taken a fresh dog with us. We had the net down at the corner of a large
field were the road cut through. I left my wife with the net as the dogs
had killed a hare, and not bein shure of the new one I went to get it.
Wen I come back towards the road I met her comen up to meet me. She
said while she was waiten she herd some one comen close to her, she could
hear them the other side of the hedge, and she had had to leave the net.
We drew towards the hedge and listened and presently heard some one
go bang on the ground, and heard him sware. . . . He got up and turned
on his lamp to se if there was anything lyen about, but there was only the
net, the wife had brought the hare away and left the net. We heard him
say quite plainly 'Its that dam——!'

Well I met the Police man a day or so after and had the cheek to ask
him if he had hurt his hands in the fall. He had my net all right, but he
was a good sort, and gave it me back for a hare.

The Police used to bother us a bit at times. Some days they came quite
frendly, and wanted to know wich way I was on such a night, and did
I hear or se any one as there were some fowls stollen. Some times they
came and told me that they had some information about me and should
arrest me and serch the house. I only laughed at them, and told them to
serch all they liked they were welcome.

Once they came to me for some ducks that were missing, and serched
the house for them. I had a lot of rabbitts and a hare or two hung up in
the back'us, and my nets dryen on a line. They wanted to know how I
come by them, so I said the rabbitts run in the house and I shut the door
on them, and ofered to sell them a pair—rabbitts not hars, I knew bettern
that, or they would have had me all rite for sellen game with out a licence.

I had lerned a lot of law by then and knew what the Police could do
as well as they did. I could have given them a lot of information if I had
liked, as I have met men many a time wen I have been walking by night

that have been after fowels and other things. But as they did not concern me I left them alone, as I did not care what other men did.

I dont know if the Police found there ducks that time, but on a nother ocasion the Police man went to a house were he knew they had the ducks that were missing, and turned the whole place up side down. The Woman that was sitting there had a baby in a cradle, and the ducks were under it, but he never thought to look under the baby. They used to call him Cradle after that but he never knew what it meant.

Then some thing hapened wich made them verry careful how they handled me. A Farmer lost some Tur-keys, and they took me and my pall and locked us up on suspicion. They took me first and then they went after him, and said that I had told them everything. Wen he came to the lock up he asked me what I had told them. Of corse I said nothing as I knew nothing about the Turkeys.

Well they took us befor the Mager-strates and remanded us for eight days to se what they could make out. Just befor we were to apear again they found the Turkeys under a straw stack that had fallen over. They let us out with a lot of Apologies but that did not sute me. I went to a Lawyer to know what redress I could get. I put the case in his hands and he got 5£ each for us for rongful arrest.

That tale had a finish to it. A Game Dealer at Lynn wanted to know if I could get some Pea Fowl, or eggs. I had noticed this same Lawyer had a lot of them Birds—they used to sit and lay about the place. I took a dark lantern one night, and hunted round and come acros a bird sitten on some eggs. I put the old bird in a bag and the eggs in my shirt. Then I come acros another bird with young ones, they too went in the bag, and I got them safley to the Dealers and made a good days work out of them. So much for his helping us, but he helped himself as well I'm thinking.

Still I most found it best to be sivell to the Police and give them sivell answers if I could, and they mostly knew wen to leave off asken me questions. They could not get near my door, as we always had a dog chained up on each side of the path so no one could pass. They had to be careful, and if I was not at home wen they come, they had to wait till I come home, as my wife would never let any one near the door if she was alone.

Wen the dogs were chained up in there kennels the ground was swept as far as they could reach for fear of poison. We knew there were many that would have liked to have finished the dogs off for us if they could, but we were to fly for them.

I never had only one dog Poisoned, but the cats used to die misterious like round our place, so we used evry precaution. The dogs were

always led out and led home, and evry bit of the ground kept swept round there shelters.

The dogs were a great protection and I never had but one that I could not train and manage, and that was a great brindle dog that I bought in Lynn market. Him I could do nothing with —he would catch a hare all rite, but soon as it was caught he had it torn to bits and eaten. I soon shot him, it is the only way with that sort, that will not lern.

There was an odd thing hapened with one of the dogs that I will tell about.

CHAPTER 6

DITTY

(SUNG FACETIOUSLY WHEN HEN-ROOSTS WERE ROBBED)

Dame, what makes your ducks to die?
What the pize[1] ails 'em, what the pize ails 'em?
Dame, what makes your chicks to cry?
What the pize ails 'em now?

For there is one goes hitch, and another goes lame,
What the pize ails 'em, what the pize ails 'em?
And another goes huckle-back like my dame,
What the pize ails 'em now?

Dame, what makes your ducks to die?
What the pize ails 'em, what the pize ails 'em?
They kick up their heels, and there they lie,
What the pize ails 'em now?

Dame, what ails your ducks to cry?
Heigh, ho! Heigh, ho!
Dame what ails your ducks to die?
Eating o' Polly-wigs[2] now.

Dame, put on your holliday gown
And follow 'em lightly, follow 'em lightly;
And follow 'em lightly through the town,
Heigh, ho! now.

Traditional in Norfolk, Suffolk,
and Cambridge

[1] 'What the pize', a form of the expression 'What the pest'.
[2] 'Polly-wigs' or 'Polly-wogs', earwigs.

CHAPTER 6

Yesterday I loved,
Today I suffer,
Tomorrow I die.
But I shall gladly
Today and tomorrow
Think on yesterday.

From the German

M Y wife had a dog of her own called Tip, that she was a lot set on, a blue dog with a fair amount of coat and a lovly brown eye. He was a cross between a Smithfield[1] and a Greyhound, Smithfield on the mother's side Greyhound on the father's and he had all the Smithfield sence and the Greyhound speed as most dogs of this breeding have—they are hard to beat.

He was a splendid dog, but verry little use for the Gate net, as he was to fast and would more often than not kill the hare befor it could get to the net. He was best in the wood, where if you was out with the gun he would catch a bird befor it hit the ground hardly, and would find them for you in the trees beside. He would whine if he had nothing to do, but knock them down and I or his Mistress had them straight away, but mostly her, as he knew then he would get a pice of suggar. He was good on the road too and would go along well ahead, and find out if there was any one about and come back and warn us with a growl.

---

[1] The Smithfield cattle-dog, small collies seen with drovers at all cattle markets, etc. They are onsidered to be the most intelligent, teachable, and hardy dogs, and largely used as a cross with he greyhound for producing lurchers for running rabbits and hares.—L. R. H.

57

I have had others like that and it is a strange thing how they get to know their enimies. I rember once wen we were out one night, and had had some luck, we had to leave the hars under a hedge, as there was some of our frends the Police about. I think there were five hars, and Tip went back while we waited, and fetched evry one to us one at a time. The Police were quite near but they never saw him or us.

My wife thought the world of Tip, and I often used to say to her in fun, you think more of the dog than you do of me. She looked after them all, but he was always the first to have a hot drink and a rub down wen we came in from a night's work. He would lie at her feet and look at her, and she would talk to him as she would have talked to a child, and I beleve he knew what she said as well as I did. Perhaps her feeling the way she did for that dog had some thing to do with what hapened after.

The months went by and it came to about three months befor her time. She had to give up going out with me as she always had done, as she could not get about as well as she used because of the child that was comen. So I went out alone one night and took Tip with me and lost him. Of corse I did not pay much regard to that, as dogs often miss there Master at night, but are shure to find him or go home on there owen.

Wen I got home to her in the morning time the first thing she said to me was 'Where is Tip, you have not brought him back with you?' I said no, and told her that I had missed him some were, but she need not fret as he would be home on his owen befor long. Then she said 'No, he will not come home any more, he is dead and lay on Narbrough park at the foot of a tree—I saw him hit the tree'.

Well of corse I pooed that and told her she must have been dreaming, but she said no, she had never been asleep all night but lyen and waiting for me to come home.

Well as the dog did not come back I went to look for him, and shure enough after a bit I found him as she had said layen at the foot of a large

I found him as she had said, laying at the foot of a large oak tree.

oak Tree. He had made to kill at a rabbitt and struck his head on the bole of the tree, and broke his neck.[1]

I have often wondred what was the real truth of it, and if she did see the dog die, or dreamed it.[2] I have never herd of such a thing befor or since,

[1] I have seen my bull-terriers do the same thing but not so hard as to hurt themselves permanently.—L. R. H.

[2] The following may be of interest, being a copy of part of a letter written by my father, Sir Rider Haggard, to The Times, July 21st, 1904. This letter and Sir Oliver Lodge's reply, etc., were included in the Journal of the Society for Psychical Research, October 1904. I may add that the occurrence made so great an impression on my father, that, although a keen sportsman and an excellent shot, he never again killed any animal or bird for sport to the day of his death (fish excepted).

'On the night of Saturday, July 9th, I went to bed about 12 and suffered from what I took to be a nightmare. I was awakened by my wife's voice calling to me from her bed the other side of the room. I dreamed that a black retriever dog, a most amiable and intelligent beast called Bob, the property of my eldest daughter, was lying on its side amongst brushwood or rough growth of some sort, by water. In my vision the dog was trying to speak to me in words, and failing, transmitted to my mind in an undefined fashion, the knowledge that it was dying. I woke to hear my wife asking me why on earth I was making those horrible noises. I replied I had a nightmare about a fearful struggle, and that I had dreamed old Bob was in a dreadful way, and was trying to talk and tell me about it. Thinking the whole thing was only a disagreeable dream, I made no enquiries about the dog and never even learned that it was missing till that Sunday night, when my little girl told me so. Then I remembered my dream, and the following day enquiries were set on foot.

'To be brief, on the morning of Thursday the 14th, my servant Charles Bedingfeld and I discovered the body of the dog floating in the Waveney against a weir about a mile and a quarter away.

'On Friday 15th I was going into Bungay, and was hailed by two platelayers. These men informed me that the dog had been killed by a train, and took me on a trolly down to a certain openwork railway bridge which crosses the water between Ditchingham and Bungay, where they showed me evidence of its death.

'It appears that about seven o'clock on the Monday morning, one of them, Harry Alger, was on the bridge, where he found a dog's collar torn off and broken by the engine (Bob's collar), coagulated blood and bits of flesh, of which remnants he cleaned the rails. I also found portions of black hair. On the Monday afternoon and subsequently his mate George Arterton saw the body of the dog floating in the water beneath the bridge, whence it drifted down to the weir, it having risen with the natural expansion of gases which might be expected in hot weather within about forty hours of death.

'It would seem that the animal must have been killed by an excursion train that left Ditchingham at 10.25 on Saturday night. This was the last train which ran that night; no trains run on Sunday....

'From traces left upon the piers of the bridge it appears that the dog was knocked or carried along some yards by the train, and fell into the brink of the water where reeds grow. Here if it were still living (but the Veterinary thinks that death was practically instantaneous), its life may but so it was. I little thought then of the trouble that was comen to me, and that I was so soon to lose her as well.

She was a strong and healthy girl of twenty two and had never ailed anything to speak of, and looked as if she would live for many years, wich perhaps acounts for why I never thought of such a thing as losing her.

The days went on till the time come for her confinement, wen to my great sorrow she died. Young as I was then it was the hardest blow I have ever had to bear in all my life, the more so because it came so sudden, and there was no reason I knew it should all end like that, and no warning. She did not want to go and I had lost a dear pall as well as a loven wife, and she had left me with a new born baby—for the child, a boy, lived.

I had to go on liven with out her, and could scarcely beleve it at first. I missed her so for many a year, and many a night wen I have been out on the Job, I have laid quiet behind a hedge wen the dogs have been worken a field, and fancied I have herd her laugh beside me, and say—'Here they come' as she used to do.

Well I supose that I got more careless after I had lost her, life did not mean much, and I did not seam to care what hapened to me. The more daring the Job that I took on hand the better it suited me, as it seamed to make me forget.

Perhaps if I had beleved diffrent about her I should have felt diffrent. Do not think that I am an Infidel, far from that, but though I was brought up religus I could not think all they said was right. The bigest fool on earth must know that there is something we can never onderstand about

perhaps have lingered for a few minutes, it must have suffocated and sunk, undergoing, I imagine, much the same sensations as I did in my dream, and in very similar surroundings, namely amongst a scrubby growth at the edge of water.

'I am forced to conclude that the dog Bob, between whom and myself there existed a mutual attachment, either at the moment of his death, if his existence can have been conceivably prolonged till after one in the morning, or as seems more probable, about three hours after that event, did succeed in calling my attention to its actual or recent plight, by placing whatever portion of my being is capable of receiving such impulses when enchained by sleep, into its own terrible position.'

this world. If any one go out and look about him at the stars, the moon, the sun, the earth and all that there is in the earth, he must know that there is some thing more than mere man.

I have read the writings of Tom Paine, and Charles Bradlawe and many other books on the subject. Some call them fools, but I say they are the clevrest men I have read of. None of them deniy that there is some Supreme bein over us, some thing that rule the lives of men, and rule the world. I do not think any one can deniy that—but I do not think there is an after Life for man—why should there be.

We have no means of knowing. I am a beliver in Fate and have been ever since I begun to think for myself. I think that Fate have played a good part in my life—or is it a case of the Devell take care of his owen? I beleve that fate rule our lives from our Births to the grave. I do not think that lots of People can help what they do.

Still I do beleve that a man who has always lived an upright life, and hurt no one by word or deed that he could help, it is better for him wen he come to the last. He can leave this world with a Clear concince, and die hapier than the man that have ofended against the laws of the supreme Bein, and against the laws of man. He that have done that have more fears of death than the upright man, but its a hard road is life for some to follow, and none are perfect, no not one.

Did not Christ tell us that we all have sined, and come short of the Glory of God.

. . . . .

So things went on much the same way as befor, the same and yet so diffrent. I had not even the child wich might have been company and a comfort, as my old Mother had taken him to bring up.

Strange to say I did not care for the baby, much as I had loved his mother. Evry time that I thought of him I could not but think how he had been the death of her—I know it was foolish on my part and may be wrong, but there it was. I suppose the love that I had for my wife blinded me to what he might have been to me if I had brought him up my self. He was all I had left of her, and the happiness she had given me, but as I never had much to do with him I thought less and less of him. Poor boy he never knew much of a Father's love, and his Grandmother had to be both father and Mother to him, which she was to the end for he never come back to live with me.

CHAPTER 7

THE FARMER'S PLOUGHBOY

One day a brisk young Farmer
Was ploughing of his land,
He called unto his horses
And bid them gently stand.

He set himself upon a gate
A song for to sing,
Making hills and valleys
With melody to ring.

Singing of a pretty damsel,
Nutting in the wood;
His song it so beguiled her
It charmed her where she stood.

So much it pleased her
She could no longer stay;
All the nuts that she had got
She was forced to throw away.

She went unto young Johnny,
These words to him did say,
'Your song it has so charmed me
I could no longer stay'.

He put his arms about her,
Sat her gently on the ground;
Said she, 'Young man, I think I see
The world go round and round'.

Then said young Johnny, 'Your mother
Will think you stay too long';
She said, 'Young man pray again
Make the world go round with your song'.

Now then, my pretty maidens,
A warning take by me,
Or you will have a jolly young ploughboy
To dance upon your knee.

Traditional: Obtained from the Author in MS.

CHAPTER 7

Come, come, Mr. Gunner,
Prythee, Mr. Gunner,
A little more powder
Your shot doth require,
Fire, Gunner, fire, do, do.

Come, come, my brave boys,
This is rarely well done,
This is the firing of the gun,
Fire, Gunner, do, do.

Traditional:
From *The Suffolk Garland*

WEN the game was out that year I turned my atention to the egg
trade, wich can be verry payen if you know were to place them.
I have lain in the wood all night and even gone onto the Keeper's door
step for them befor now. Of corse getten the eggs away safe was by far
the worst of that Job, so I had to resort to all kinds of tricks.

I rember once buyen a large old accordion and taken the inside out,
and packen all the eggs in that. Then I gave it to the Carrier to take into
Lynn, and met him there and took the eggs to the Dealers. Well one day
wen I was on this Job I met a Farmer that knew me and had a grudge
agin me I supose, any how he put the Police on my track. A Police man
came up to me and told me that he suspected me of haven game eggs in
my posession, and that he shold take me to the Police Station and serch
me.

Well as I had got away from the Dealers and knew they would find nothing I did not make any trubble about that, and went willing enough as I was thinking what a surprise I had in store for him. Wen we got there the Police Sargeant wanted to know what the charge was. Wen the Police man told him and started to take the cover from the Musical, the end come off, and all he found inside was saw dust.

The Sargeant wanted to know what I was goen to do with it,—I told him that I was goen to get new tunes in it as he was too late for the old ones.

By that time I had several pounds saved, so I was inderpendent of any one, and no one could say nothing whatever I chose to do.

There was a verry clever Keeper come to the next villige about this time, and he used to boast that he had forty hen Pheasants under wire. He knew all about my Job, and he used to tell People he would get me befor the year was out. Of corse I sone got to know that he had the birds there. He used to talk a lot and tell People that no one could get at them as he had a dog tied up and an alarm gun set.

It was not long before I had hatched a plan. I got a chap to go to him and ask if he had any ferrits to sell, and told him to keep his eyes open and look round to se were the gun was fixed. He did and brought me back word of the exact tree that the gun was screwed onto.

Well first of all I set to work to find a market, as I had made up my mind to get them birds, and I sone found one about four miles away. The next thing to do was to get a bitch in use wich I did, and took with me and let her run, wich is an old trick, and verry usful wen you have a dog to deal with. I soon found the gun and put that right, and then cut a hole in the wire and got evry one of them Birds. I did not do that Job alone but two of us did—we got safe away to the road, and the Birds were at there new home befor they were missed.

Of course the rout was out, and a lot of enquires were made, and they came and serched my Place, but as there were neither Birds nor Feathers, they were lost to know what to do. I got just on five pounds for them Birds that trip.

I was thinking what a surprise I had in store for them.

On another ocasion there were a Clever Chap, and he got thorns and all the Busshes he could colect, and made Burrers for Rabbitts on a medaw. Then he bought a lot of tame rabbitts and got some wild ones to run with them—in fact they Bread verry fast. Well he was goen to have all the Publicans and Shop keepers down on Boxing Day to turn the place over and he stood to make a bit out of it. He watched this place and the Rabbitts verry carefully, but a day or so befor Christmas, we got bussy and went and put the nets round that field, and scopped the lot. Of corse they all come as arranged and turned the Place over but the game was gone, and that chap had a good bit to say.

I got the creditt for it as I did for evry other Job at that time, wether I was in it or not, but as the Rabbitts were at Lynn that all fell through. Do not think Dear Reader, from what I have told you, that every sckeme came off that I tried for, far from it. I must tell you how I went and got into bad trubble again.

About that time I was training a young Lurcher Dog, and I did train him, so he was clever as a man in most things. Me and this dog and a seven yard net, have killed hundreds of hars and rabbitts, but I will tell more of my dogs and how I train them later. One day the Keeper swore that the dog killed a hare wich was a lie that time—but of cors I had to pay. I told him then that I would take as many pounds off the estate as I had paid shillings—and so I did. I worked that place for all I was worth.

One night I was out and had the net up close to his house, were the hars used to come over the road way. Wile I was waiten I saw him comen, but I had no time to get the net away. I got behind a bush and as he come past me I laid him out with a crack, and he never knew who hit him. Well I never had any more trubble with him after that, as I think he thought he might be done in if he was found out again. Of corse there was a great stir about it, but as he did not know who hit him that blew over; but he always thought that I was the man.

But I did not always get off like that. I was in a wood one night, and had had a few shots wen I walked into four Keepers. Of corse I knew I was beat that time, I had not a chance and was wiling to give in, but they knocked me about with sticks and kicked me most onmercifull. Then they got a cart from the farm near by, and took me to the lock up and left me.

The next morning I was nearly Dead, so bad that the Police had to send for the Doctor, and wen he had looked at me he ordered me to be taken to Lynn Ospitall. I had a verry bad cut head and a Brused Boddy.

I stayed there for a fortnight, and wen I was able to get about and got my Discharge, a Policeman was waiting for me and I had to go back to Grimstone Lock up. My head was still bandged up, and wen the Maderstrates saw me I think they had some pitty, as they asked me if I wold be tried there or go to the Sessions. As I had only a week to wait I went to the Sessions.

Well wen it come to it the Keepers swore that I had put up a terrible fight—theretned to shoot them and all that. The Judge did not beleve them, but as I was Poaching I had to get it, but he let me off with twenty one days, and told the Keepers that they had behaved verry cruele to me. I was sent back to Norwich—to the New Prison on Mousehold this time, but they gave me no task there as I was still verry sore. I think that the Judge had some thing to do with that.

Well the Head Keeper got the sack . . . he should not have allowed the other ones to have knocked me about as they did, I supose they thought that they were getten some of there own back on me, for all the tricks I had played them but that never stopped me, I was Just as eager as ever. In fact I had got such a liken for the Game I was past stoppin. Poaching is something like drug taking,—once begun no goen back, it get hold of you. The life of a Poacher is any thing but a happy one, still it is exciting at times, and the excitement go a long way to sothe his concience if it trubble him.

In the old days of sixty year ago, men were often driven to that kind o life by the Hard times. Since then some do it for the sake of sport, and

They got a cart from the farm near by, and took me to the lockup——.

the excitement of the game, that was so in my case, and a great many more beside—I loved the excitement of the Job. Beside you had the satafaction of knowen that you had got Keepers and Police beat, and that went a long way towards recompence for the danger and risk run. Of corse wen I got had, I took it as part of the Bargin, but that did not happen verry often. Some men take to the hen rost to help the bag, but a rearly good Poacher never do that, it is game he want and game he will get.

True, the Keepers get some of the tricks, but how many do the Poacher get? I venture to say that he get ninety nine out of the hundred, as the Professnial is as cunning as a fox at his Job, wen he know his Job propply, and can beat the Keeper most times. Later on I am goen to tell how some of it is done. The Professnial man is of cors an Outlaw to the Laws of the Land, and nothing but a rouge and a Vagerbond in some People's eye, but he is not so black as some people paint him—but black enough perhaps. Be that as it may, I wold soner have a night out with either gun or dog, than go to the best Diner Party ever Provided.

Of corse I have had a lot of sumones, but that did not trubble me as long as I could pay, and I supose it have cost me a Hundred pounds one time and another in fines. Wile I could keep out of Prison and keep my freedom I did not mind that.

Well I had got the name of the King of The Norfolk Poachers in them Days, and I expect I earned it. I could run like a hare once I had got a start—no one could catch me, and him who cant run cant poach.

I rember once I got disturbed at night, and had to run for it as there were two Keepers close to me, in fact it was one of them as was given me the run. I had to carry my bag and gun, but as sone as I got the chance I dropped the bag in a ditch, and made for the river Nar. I Jumped in and got out on the other side, as the Keepers landed on the other Bank, so I got the laugh of them again and a good ducking into the Bargain, but that did not matter. I went back in the early morning and retreved my bag and game, as they never knew that I had dropped it.

I never felt any anomosity for a keeper or a Policeman if he got me fair and square and told no lies, as the Defendant know if they are lyen better than any one else. I know that they have there duty to do, and it was up to me to do mine and circumvent them if I could.

Well once there hapened to be a Pigeon shoot, and it was that there Pigeon shoot wich led to all the trubble. Befor I tell about that I might say that I was verry much intrested in that kind of sport and was often called upon to procure Birds. There was a Gentleman Farmer at ower place, and he had some young Ladies who were verry fond of Pigeons, they used to keep them in Barrells made into Pidgeon Cotes.

The night befor some of these shoots, me and a Pall used to take a net on poles, and put it round them barrells and capture most of the Birds. That was not stealing, as some of them used to fly back,—them that did not get killed. In fact we used to raid any Pigeon Cote that we hapened to know of, some times goen sevrell miles for them, not for there value, but more for shere sport.

Well to go back to this Petacular match. It was about three miles from home, and of cors we had to go walking as Bycicliss were not so numeriss as they are to day. I did well at that Pigeon shoot, and won a duble Breach Loding gun that day, and wen we were all comen home at night one of us spied a Phesant on a tree. No sooner seen than it was dead, and that started us off. I suppose we had all had a merry time and were verry well pleased with ourselves, any ways we soon got bussy in the wood.

That was all right, but things bein what they were we were not as careful as we should have been and I expect made a bit of a racket. Two Keepers must have heard us and they come along and was on us befor we knew. One of my mates sone laid one of them out, and I had the plesure of stoppin the other one. He hapened to be the man as had treated me so bad befor, and as by that time we was well in it, I did not stop to think or lose the chance of payen some of the score back that I owed.

Well the Game was up then for me, and I knew I must get away as quick as I could, or they would be onto me, as I was thinking we had hurt both them Keepers verry badly and were in for a lot of trubble soon as they was found. So I got to the nearest town and into the train for the North of England, before many hours were past.

Of corse there was a warrent out for me in no time but as I had got clean away to the City of Manchester I was safe. I had another name, and it seam we had not hurt the Keepers as much as I expected, so the Police did not bother about me as long as I was gone.

I rember well that was the year of the Jublee, the first of Victoria's Reign, and I stayed there in Manchester six years.

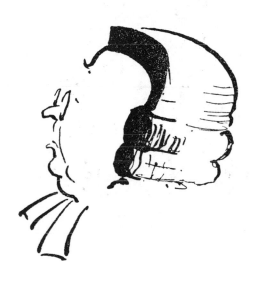

CHAPTER 8

THE CONVICT SHAMROCK GREEN

A constant girl was heard to cry
And wipe the tears from out her eye,
Saying, 'The cruel laws of Our Gracious Queen—
They have transported my Shamrock Green.

'For being unruly I do declare
That seven long years was hardly fair;
There were seven links in his shackling chain,
One for each year across the main.'

Six of the years were gone and past,
We had set sail to make the last,
The stormy winds did blow and roar,
And cast me on this foreign shore.

The Convict landed his little boat
Which on the ocean with him did float.
The birds at night take their silent rest,
But the Convict carried a wound in his breast.

The Coast Guard waited on the beach
Till the Convict's boat was within his reach.
Though the day be far gone and the night advance—
You have a friend in the Coast of France.

'God bless that Coast Guard', the Convict cried,
'Who has rescued me from the ocean wide,
I drink his health in a flowing glass,
And here is success to the Coast of France.'

A letter was sent to her Gracious Queen,
About the loss of Shamrock Green;
A reprieve was sent by a speedy hand
To summon the Convict to his native land.

Obtained in MS. from the Author.

CHAPTER 8

He travels safest in
the dark of the night
who travels lightest

CORTEZ

I LANDED up in Manchester late at night, not knowen a bit of the place
or any one there, and to add to that I was expecten a Police man's hand
on my shoulder at any time—and that is no pleasant feeling to live with.
But it seam I had given them the slip, or perhaps they never trubbled
about me as long as I had gone away.

I well rember goen out of the Centrell Station at Manchester, and asken
a Police man were I could get Lòdgens. He took me to a quiet Hotel in
New Bridge Street, close to Victoria Station, and there I spent the rest of
the night none to easy in my mind.

The next day I went to look for a Job. Bein strange I did not know
were to start and look, till I found a free Libriry, and looken through
the papers saw an advertizement for a man wanted at a Horse dealers.
It was not much in my line it was true, but why not me as well as a
nother, so I aplied and got the Job. The Stables were at the back of the
Strangways Prison, and there I worked for some time.

The next thing was to let my Mother know were I had got to, as I was
thinken they must be in a pretty state about me at home. Of corse I had
another name in Manchester, but I had a frend at Lynn, that used to buy
game of me in the old days, and through him I used to get letters home.

I dont say as how I liked it much at the Horse Dealers, but Jobs that I
could do were not easy to come by, and I stuck to it and got used to it,

as one can most things. My Master was a good Master to me, and I always got a good tip wen he made a good deal, but I just did not like the Job.

He used to go over to Ireland and buy half broken carriage horses there, and then bring them back and break them to harness, and drive them about the town of Manchester in dubbile and single Harness all silver

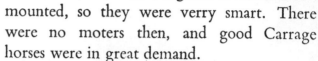

mounted, so they were verry smart. There were no moters then, and good Carrage horses were in great demand.

He took me to Ireland with him three times, so I saw a bit of the Cuntry and the buyen over there. We used to buy from the Farmers and at the Horse Fairs. The Irish Fair is a good bit diffrent from the English Fair, as there is a great absence of plesure—no Roundbouts, and that sort of thing, the three Card Trick, and Pricking the Garter are the chief amusments. There is plenty of drinken and some fighten, that is among them selves, for the Irish are ever corteous to a Stranger.

I rember well the Horse Fair at a place called Armar. There is no ring there to show the horses, they are all run up and down the Fair among the people, with a lot of shouting and whip cracking. I was greatly pussled by one of there cries, it sounded like 'Faugh a Baller'—I asked an Irishman what it meant and he said it was 'Clear the Way' in there language.

There was a lot of other things sold at them fairs, Donkeys by hundreds, and geese and ducks. You would see the little bare foot boys and girls runing round and round the flocks of geese and duck, keeping them in bunches. Then there was the cows and calves brought along in great number, but as ower Job was horses, I did not get much chance to look at them.

'Faugh, a Baller!'

The women had a lot to say at the sale of the horses. The horses that are reared by the Irish farmers and there wives are mostley verry quiet as they are petted from foals. Some times out would come the farmer's wife in the middle of the deal, and tell him he 'Must not sell that pretty creature as she had brought up by hand, for surely it would break her heart to part with it', and then wipe her eyes and make a lot of to do until they got the money for the horse safe, and the deal finished.

An Irishman do not forget to ask enough, but my Master was a canna Scotsman, and I have often smiled wen he was bargining for a horse. The owner would ask a long price, and my Master would say I will give you so much—it may be worth it to you but not to me, and the Irish-man would start comen down. He went on comen down usually till he got to my Master's price, for I think he always gave what the horse was worth to him.

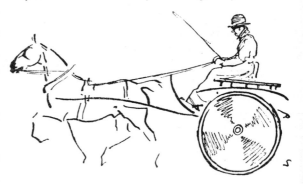

There are a great many horses at them fairs wich are fifteen hands or over—what he wanted was horses of fourteen hand, or there abouts. The great object was to get horses to match in pairs, he did not mind if one should hapen to have a white patch or star, that was easley altered—two or three dressings with Corestick would sone change that. He did not care what he give if onley they matched in dubble harness, wen they would be worth any thing from a Hundred pound up to him. You must onderstand dear Reader that there were a lot of verry rich Manufactures in Manchester, and all were tryen to out do each other as regards Carradge Horses—no motter cars in them days.

Once bought my Job was to lead the horses away to Newtown or Dublin, which ever was the nearest to us, ready for the boat. They were stabbled there to wait till we had nine or ten to ship to Liverpool.

I used to think Dublin was a lovley place, and looken across the Bay to the Wicklow mountains is most beautifful, they look there best from there with the morning sun on them.

In fact Ireland is a Beautifful country—pitty there is so much onrest there, but most of it is riligon that cause the bother. I always found the Irish homely, good natured, and civell to a stranger.

I was in Ireland again in 1919, I was tellergramed for as my son, that was the son of my second wife, was verry ill on the Currar Camp with newmonia, and they did not think that he would live. I was there with

him six weeks, and went a long way about Ireland, and found the same thing as I had done before. The Irish People were always ready to give you a welcome. If I went to house and asked for a drink of water, they would

offer a drink of butter-milk, or a cup of tea, or some home made wine. They were verry fond of hearing how we went on in England, and wanted to know a lot about English ways and would have you sit and tell them by the hour, in them small cabins wich are scattred about in hundreds all over the Cuntry.

They seam to be so poor, do the Irish, yet most of them have a cow and a cupple of pigs, and some fowles, and I fancy they are not so poor as they look. Neither beleve me is the Irishman so dunce as he is taken to be, not by a long way—he is any thing but a fool.

My Boy got well again I am thankful to say, and is still in the Army, but there I am goen many years ahead of them days, wen I was with the Horse Dealer.

Wen we had got about ten horses we had to ship them to Liverpool.

It was a terrible Job loading them on the boat at Dublin, half broke as they were and frightened out of there lives by the strangness. They were run on bord, and led down into the hold, and there put into a kind of box, wedged in so they could not stir or lay down. I rember one time the Channell was verry rough, comen over to Liverpool, and it was a terrebble Job all together. Some times the horses were on there heads and some times strait up from there hind legs, and I had to be between them all the way over. I have often wondred why I never got hurt, but I did not, and one thing was my Master would never send me were he would not go himself.

Wen they were safe landed we had to rail them to the Centrell Station Manchester, and get them home to be licked into shape and got ready for the Carrage of some big Manafacturer. If they were not good enough for that they were sold to the Manchester Tramway Company.

I rember well one mare he bought a beautifful bay Mare, he got her at the fair in Armar. Wen he got her home and put her in a braik she would not budge an inch. My Master tried all sorts of plans with her, some were cruell, and some were kindness but not one was any use. At last he put her in a heavy cart, and she stood there two days and nights. She was tied so she could not stir head or legs, and wen we let her go at liberty she fell down. There we let her laye till she got up her selfe, and from that day she was never any more trubble. I beleve he sold her for a Hundred Pound.

· · · · ·

Well time went on and I begun to know my way about in Manchester, and used to go to a Public house on the Cheetmill Road. I found there were a sporting lot of men there, and a Pigeon shooting Club, and all sorts of other sports. Of corse wen I first went they were very anxous to know a bit about me, and also if I could handle a gun. I told them as much as suted me and they named me Cockney, thinking I came from London.

The first match that I was shooten in was at the Three Arrows on the Middleton Road at the corner of Eaton Park, the seat of Lord Eaton. I

believe he have thrown it open as a Public Park now. I was picked out
for one of the contestin team,—we were shooten a team from Besses of
the Barn. I rember well the Manchester team won the match—I think it
was ten birds each—and that I killed every bird with a single shot, it being
in my line so to speak.

The pigions were put in what was called fall traps, so wen the trapper
pulled the string the trap fell flat. We used to shoot twenty yards rise for
Pigions, and forty yards fall, that is to say the bird had to fall within the
forty yards of the trap.

When they shot for sparows they were eighteen yards rise and thirty
yards fall. If a Pigion refused to flie the Guner could walk up to it until
it did flie, or if the Pigion flew a yard from the trap the Guner could kill
it on the ground.

The Sweepstakes were half a crown and eight pence a Pigion, no
Profesnialls alowed to shoot. I won many a sweep at that game, but it
was a verry expencive sport if you did not get first or second prize, but
I do not think I ever lost money by that Job.

Well after that they all wanted to know a lot, more than I cared to tell
them, about were I lived and were I worked; still I got on all right with
them. Most of them were Colliers and factory Hands. Time went on, and
it come about that I felt I wanted to change my Job, seeing it was seven
days a week, and worken for a horse dealer were not what I cared about.
So one of my palls, a forman at some print works, got me a Job at his
place, a mill Called Booker Bank at Crumpshall, and there I worked the
rest of the time I was in Lancashire.

I found that Child Labour was there too. You would see little chaps
goen with there fathers to the Coal pit, carrien there tin food box and tea
can. They went down in the pits at a verry early age and were called
Trappers, that is to say they had to sit beside a canvas door, and open it
for the skips drawn by the pit ponies to pass through, and then close it
after them. The object was to stop the coal dust from getten in the
workings, and keep the good air in the lower seams of coal.

On the top you would see plenty of young girls picken Cole. As it was brought to the top it was shot into screens and then the girls picked the pices of slate and rock out as it slid down the screens. That was what was called Hand picked cole; we do not se much of that down this way.

I went down a pit once one afternoon, the first and last time they ever got me down one of them places. It was called Pin Mill pit, belongen to the Clifton and Kersley Company. I was friendly with the Foreman and he fixed it. They gave me a sute of Over Alls, and I got into the cage with the other men with the safty lamp in my hand and my matches and pipe

all took away from me. The bell rang and down we went—and a most horrible feeling it is, some thing like Jumping from the top of a high tower or steeple must be, your whole inside seams to lose its moorings and come up inside your throat.

The pit was eight Hundred feet deep, but we seam to be there as soon as we started, perhaps because I would have sooner been some were else. Wen we arived at the botom wich is called the Sump, I with the other Colliers got into one of the small skips and were carried to the face of the Cole, drawn by the pit ponies. The little pit boys were set down as we came to the canvas doors, to set there in the dark for eight hours on end.

Wen we arived at the Cole face I was told I could go up any gallary

G

were I could hear the sound of the pick at work. There was a terrible explosion in this pit the year before I went down, and I believe there were close on one hundred men and boys killed. Every now and then as you went along you could se a name chalked up at diffrent spots. I wanted to know what they meant and then they told me that was the place were diffrent men were picked up dead, killed by the After Damp, not very cheerful I did'nt think, but then I had no liken for cole mines.

I staid down till the four hour men came up, and I came up with them and glad I was to get out of it, being fed up with mines and all to do with them. You would think wen you were down there you were in a large wood with the props standing about—thousands of them. You would hear them burst like the crack of a whip, but there were always men there to put in fresh ones at once. There was a continuall drip of water evrywere, and the cole Hewers worked with nothing on except a pair of ragged trousers and Clogs. I know I was whet through and as black as any collier wen I got to the top, resolved never to go down a cole mine again if I knew it.

Of corse I Joined in the Sports of the Colliers and mill workers, and they did a lot in that line up there. I did not care for some such as Rat corsen and Pigeon flying, but I was fond of Whippet racing, and brought out a good Whippet and won a lot of corses with him.

The way with the whippets was this. A man would go about two Hundred yards down the set course and held a white hancurcheif in his hand. The Slipper who was holding the dogs would get them ready and at the crack of the pistoll the dogs were let go, there owners waved the hancurcheif and the dogs raced for them, the one that got there first winning the heat. Of corse they were trained to that from Pups. The Stakes were not verry high but there was money to be won at that game, and it was all sport with the lads.

Corsen rats was some thing like corsen rabbitts, except that they were not put in traps. The rats were brought in cages, and a man would take a rat from the cage, show it to the terriers, and then carry it about thirty yards. The dogs were held in slips the same as for racen whippitts, and wen the dogs were ready the man with the rat would let it go. The first dog that picked up the rat won the heat and so it would go on until the two best dogs were run together at the last. The Prise might be a copper Kittle or some other usefull article. Of corse there was a lot of betting on the diffrent dogs, that was the sport of the game.

Not haven been used to it I did not care much for that kind of sport, the gun was always what I liked the best, but I used to go to keep in with the rest of the Boys.

There was a place in Ancoats were they used to have Cock fights and Dog fights, but there I never went though I might have done had I liked. I have never been a religus man but I did not care for that sort of sport on a Sunday morning. There are some funny places in Lancashire—the Workmen's Clubs were Members could get drinks all day, but no Stranger was alowed to pay any thing, the member was supposed to treat him if he took a Stranger there.

I have been taken to some queer showes some times with some of the boys, no one would Credit the places that are found in some of the back streets of that citty. It used to take a good bit to shock me in them days, haven knocked about as I had, but I have been glad to get out of some of them. And they are the same lads as will take a bird in a cage and walk miles with it on there arm to give the bird some air.

Still I have always found them a good class of men and there is no reason in expecting all the world to think the same way as you do. Wen they got to know you in a Generall way they are honest and good natured, and I can safely say I was always treated with the greatest respect no matter how rough the company.

I did not save much money there as there was a lot to spend it on. Wages were good, but there was outings in plenty in the summer, and Working men's Clubs. So one way and another I made myself more or less content, and got plenty of sport and Excitement, which kept me from thinking too much of what I had lost before I went to Manchester. Although I did not think much about my boy, I rote home to Mother regular, and sent her money for his keep.

So six years passed, and then my Mother wrote to me that she wanted me to come back home, as my Father was failing fast. Also I had had word that one of the Keepers that I had been in trubble with was dead, and the other one gone away, and I did not think that being so they would renue the warrant out against me. So I made up my mind to go back to the old Place again and face the musick.

CHAPTER 9

HARVEST HEALTHS

The Master's Good Health

Here's a health unto our Master, the founder of the Feast,
I wish with all my heart and soul in Heaven he may find rest.
I hope all things may prosper, that ever he takes in hand,
For we are all his servants, and all at his command.
Drink, boys, drink, and see you do not spill;
For if you do, you must drink two, it is your Master's will.

The Mistress's Good Health

Now Harvest is ended and supper is past,
Here's to our Mistress's good health, boys, in a full and flowing glass.
She is a good woman, she prepared us good cheer,
Come all my brave boys now, and drink off your beer.
Drink, my boys, drink, till you come unto me,
The longer we sit, my boys, the merrier we shall be.

When the Ale was drunk out of doors

In yon green wood there lies an old fox,
Close by his den you may catch him or no.
Ten thousand to one you catch him or no.

His beard and his brush are all of one colour,
I am sorry, kind Sir, that your glass is no fuller (*drinks*).
'Tis down the red lane, 'tis down the red lane,
So merrily hunt the fox down the red lane.

Traditional

CHAPTER 9

There were then but two families
in the World—Havemuch and Havelittle.

Don Quixote

Come, friends, and listen to this rhyme
About the English Labour;
How he fared in the olden time
And all the ills he bore,
Until he stood up in manhood
Resolved to bear no more.
He used to tramp off to his work
While town folks lay in bed,
With nothing in his belly
But a slice or two of bread.
He used to find it hard enough
To give his children food,
And as his wages would not yeild
Enough for bread and clothes,
He had to send them to the fields
To scare away the crows.

F. R.

So I come back home again, and looked round to see what was doing befor I settled down. But I never heard of what was past, and no one made any trubble, and I begun to feel myself fairly safe.

Duren the last two years of my time in Manchester I had fallen in love with a girl that worked with me in the mill were I was Imployed. Wen

87

I had been home a month or two and found that all was quiet and I was in no trubble with the Law, I sent for her to come down to Norfolk and we were married.

I was twenty eight and she was twenty one, and I found my new wife a very easy minded girl to live with, but she found it hard to settle, not knowen my people's ways or speech, and the old folk not knowen what to make of her. It was not so easy to live with the old People at all, as my ways were not there ways, but after my marrage I found it Impossible, and soon had a home of my owen again. Then come the question of what to do, times were bad, and the Labour only got ten shilling a week, and that did not suit me. I could not make shift to live on that.

I have heard many People say, give me the good old days of fifty year ago, but beleve me there were no good old days fifty years ago, except for the man with plenty of gold. The worken classes were little better than slaves, they were worked from there Cradles to there Graves—people think that times are bad now, but they were many times worse then. Men had to tramp to work hours sooner than to day, and they got a mere pittance, nine shilling a week to bring up a family.

Some People say, ah, but things were much cheaper in them days, quite coreckt, but they were Just as dear in proportion as now, in fact more so. Scors of famleys were brought up on potatos, turnips, and Bread, with what was called Pork lard and Treackle, with a change of herring. Were they were a big famley often as not they would have to go three of them to one herring.

The Children was sent out at an early age into the fields to work, scaren crows and such like Jobs. I can well rember wen lots of poor Children had to go to work in the Spring of the year, picken foule grass, and other Jobs, from eight in the morning till five in the afternoon, some with scarse any boots on there feet. The Master would send a man to keep them at work, and he would stand in the field with a stick or whip to keep them at it. Wen they had done the day's work they would get the sum of three Pence.

A little boy was put to keep them off the stacks.

Further on in the Summer, the older ones were employed to cut thissells in the corn, I have seen as many as forty children in one field with there Task master standing over them. They would get from eighteen pence to two shilling a week, working from eight till five. They had to go to work to help keep them selves.

I have seen many a Poor woman go to the fields in bitter winter weather, cleaning turnips and beat for the cattle, for the sum of ten pence a day. They would come home up to there knees in mud and whet, and then they would have the house hold work to do, washing cooking mending, and all the other Jobs wich come along wen there is a big famley to do for, and famleys mostley were big in them days.

Small wonder that so many were crippled with rhumatics, and brought children into the World with rhumatics bread into them.

I well rember close to the Cottage were my Parents lived, a farmer had a lot of stacks of corn standing. It was sharp winter time, and they were sharp winters wen I was young. The crowes were hard set and started to pick the stacks to pieces to get at the corn. A little boy was put to keep them off the stacks—not more than seven or eight years old. The poor little chap stood there all day, and was struck by the cold; the Steward found him nearly dead, and picked him up and brought him into my Mother. She treated him as best she knew, with hot blankets, and hot bottles and hot sand, and they brought him round.

To his credit he never forgot my Mother. Wen he grew to a young man he got work on the line, and rose from Porter to Guard, on one of our fastest trains. He never missed a year but what he sent my old Mother a present at Christmas, not till the day that she died.

The Farmer that that hapened to was diffrent to a lot, and never employed child labour again all his life.

There is a lot of talk about unemployment at the present time, but there was as much in them days. In winter, wen work was slack I have seen twenty or thirty young men standing about. Lots of the Farmers would have the married men working three days a week to help them along.

I am not disparging the Farmer of them days, some were human, some did not care. There was no dole to make the young men lazy, so that they dont mind if they work or no, but there was plenty of Poaching and fowl Stealing goen on wen they were druv to it.

No use goen to the Poor Law then, no relief for them there.

So things dragged along in the same way for many years, some Farmers better than the rest would try and help. One I knew used to kill pigs and

sell them to his men at cost price, and they would pay what they could each week. Some would give them a chance digging a piece of waste land up for potatos or such like.

There was a Squire Villolas [1] liven at the next villige, Marham it was called, and he would employ all he could. He would say to his Agent, 'Cant you find them men some work, clearing out weeds, draining or any thing, if not we shall make Poachers and thieves of them all'.

Round were I was born there were some verry large fields. It was nothing to see thirty or more harvest men mowen barley [2] in one field.

[1] Henry Villebois, Esq. Died 1886.

[2] The barley 'mow' was of great importance, the barley being a valuable harvest for malting purposes, only the very highest quality being used. It had a special 'health', which was drunk to it as follows:

'Here's a health to the barley mow,
Here's a health to the man
Who very well can
Both harrow, plough and sow.
When it is well sown,
See it is well mown,
Both raked and gavell'ed * clean;
And a barn to lay it in.
Here's a health to the man
Who very well can
Both thrash and fan it clean.'
    * 'Gavell' = to place in piles.

That was long befor the time of the self binder. Harvest men got about
ix pound for there harvest then, but rents were cheaper than now,
nd many cottages were on the farms, so the Master was sure of his
ent.[1]

Harvest was a great event in them days, the great time of the whole
ear. The Farmer would call his men together wen he thought the corn
vas ripe for cutten, and tell them they would start harvest on a certain
ay. He also told them the price that he would pay them for it and they
ad no option but to agree. He would also give each man a shilling, that
vas called 'hire', and perhaps ten shilling or a pound to the rest, that was
corden to the Company of men and boys and Women. Women played

big part in the harvest field
 them days wen all was
one by hand, tiyen corn,
 d racken and other Jobs.

They had to put in a long
ay to, as there time was
om seven in the morning
ll as long as the man worked
  night. I have knowen the men to work as late as twelve O'clock at
ight on a Saturday, to get a field in, as they knew that they could rest
 the Sunday.

The ten shilling and the other odd money was what was called Wheten
er. They would go to some Public House were there was a Club Room,
 d have what they called a Shoo-ing night—that is to say if there were
 y fresh men in the Harvest who had not worked on the farm befor, or
 y young man who was doing his first harvest—then he had to be
 od.

This was done by the man who was chosen the Lord of the Harvest,
 at is to say the man who mowed first in the line of Reapers, and was

[1] Because it could be deducted from the man's wage, or else paid in some small extra service
'overtime' piece of work as is frequently done to this day.—L. R. H.

always called the Lord or Head man.[1] He would have a halter and tak
it and put it over the head of all the new men. The Lady, that is the Lad
of the Harvest, who mowed next in the line to the Lord, would then tak
a small hammer, lift the foot of a new hand and tap him on the sole of hi
boot, and he would call beer.

Wen they were all shod then they would read the Harvest rules. Tha
is certain rules that they must abide by, under the Lord of the Harvest.
a man was away for a day from his work, he was fined ten shillings, if i
was because of drink, if through bussness or famley matters he could no
come five shilling, and if because of illness onley two and sixpence. Ever
man had to keep his place in the line wen he was mowen, if he lost
swathe he was fined sixpence, or else he had to go back and get it up som
time or other.

Then there was the finish of Harvest wich was a great set out even sixt
year ago.

At most of the bigest farms, wen the last of the Corn in the last of th
Fields was cut and got up, the men would take a sheaf of wheat and tie
up and put it on a fork.[2] Then the Lord of the Harvest would hold it u

[1] The Lord of the Harvest is a custom which comes down from very early times. Sir Joh
Cullam in his *History of Hawstead* mentions 'the Head Reaper, who was annually elected an
presented to the Over Lord by the inhabitants'. In a note he remarks that the Lord of the Harve
was some old and trusted tenant who understood all harvest work and commonly led the me
reaping. The year of his office he was exempt from half his usual rents and services, and accordin
to his tenure might take his food at the table of the Manor House, if there was one, and keep h
horse in the Manor stable. He was next in dignity to the Steward and Bailiff. The Lord of th
Harvest seems to have been a well-known and established custom as early as the fourteenth century
Some idea of the extent to which labour was employed for the harvest can be gathered from th
same history, as from accounts quoted we find in the year 1388, 553 persons engaged on th
harvesting of a corn area of about 200 acres.—L. R. H.

[2] This practice is a survival of the 'Harvest Doll', 'Harvest Maiden', 'Harvest Queen', and 'Harve
Old Woman' well known all over Europe. In many of its forms (such as the one of a woman bein
wrapped in the last swathe of corn reaped, and then giving imaginary birth to a child, the puppe
being borne to the farm house amid much rejoicing), it is but the very thinly veiled worship of th
Spirit of Fertility. In the opinion of some the custom arises from the Roman feast of Ceres; othe
say it is of much greater antiquity. This custom and the habit of crying Largess to all who cam
into the harvest field, has only been killed in East Anglia in very recent years by the mechanic
reapers, which have utterly destroyed the whole ancient ceremony of the harvest.—L. R. H.

on a waggon, the men would all get in, and ride round the Master's house. They would have some times four or six horses all out at length with a man riding on each, blowen Harvest Horns, and shouting "Larges". Mostley the Farmer would come out, and pay the men, give them plenty of beer, and of cors make a bit of a speach. Then he would give the Harvest supper, and they would have a wonderful spread, with a good fat sheep, or Beef, and more Beer. Some times the supper was held in the Farmers barn and some times at a Public.

The evening was spent in merry making. The villige fidler was always there, and they would all shuffle round and sing songs, no one rembers them these days, as I do not think they was ever writen down. My old Grandmother taught them to me, The Dark Eyed Sailor, Barbra Ellen and many another that I canot rember now. Next day they would all go round to the Trades men and gather there Larges, so they mostly had two merry Nights.

All these things are past and gone now, never to be called back—more is the pitty.

CHAPTER 10

THE PLOUGHMAN'S FEASTING DAYS

This would not be slipped,
Old guise must be kept.
Good huswives, whom God hath enriched enough,
Forget not the feasts which belong to the plough;
The meaning is only to joy and be glad,
For comfort with labour is fit to be had.

Plough Monday

Plough Monday, next after that Twelfthtide is past,
Bids out with the plough, the worst husband is last;
If ploughman gets hatchet or whip to the screen,
Maids loseth their cock if no water be seen.[1]

Shrovetide

At Shrovetide to shroving, go thresh the fat hen,
If blindfold can kill her, then give it thy men;
Maids, fritters and pancakes enow see ye make,
Let slut have one pancake, for company's sake.[2]

[1] If the ploughman on Plough Monday could get any of his implements to the fireside before the maid put on her kettle she forfeited her shrovetide cock.

[2] A very old custom, quoted in some works. Hilman gives the following description:
'The hen is hung at a fellow's back, who has also some horsebells about him. The rest of the fellows are blinded and have boughs in their hands, with which they chase this fellow and his hen about some large court or small enclosure. The fellow with his hen and bells shifting as well as he can they follow the sound, and some times hit him and his hen; other times if he can get behind one of them, they thresh one another well favouredly; but the jest is the maids are to bind the fellows, which they do with their aprons, and the cunning baggages will endear their sweet-hearts with a peeping hole, whilst the others look out as sharp to hinder it. After this the hen is boiled with bacon, and a store of pancakes and fritters are made.'

Sheep-Shearing

Wife, make us a dinner, spare flesh neither corn,
Make wafers and cakes, for our sheep must be shorn;
At sheep shearing neighbours none other thing crave,
But good cheer and welcome, like neighbours to have.

The Wake-Day

Fill oven with flawns, Jenny, pass not for sleep,
Tomorrow thy father his wake-day will keep,
Then every wanton may dance at her will,
Both Tomkin with Tomlin, and Jenkin with Jill.[1]

Harvest-Home

For all this good feasting, yet art thou not loose,
Till ploughman thou givest his harvest home goose.
Though goose go in stubble I pass not for that,
Let goose have a goose, be she lean, be she fat.[2]

Seed Cake

Wife, sometime this week if that all things go clear,
An end of wheat sowing we make for this year.
Remember you therefore, tho' I do it not,
The Seed Cake, the Pasties, the Furmenty Pot.[3]

TUSSER, 1557

[1] On the night preceding the Saint's Day connected with the dedication of the Parish Church the young people of both sexes in the Parish used to keep watch in the church till morning. This led to various scandals, and was abolished; the wake or watch night taking place over the family oven, in preparation for the feast which always took place next day.

[2] At Harvest Home a goose was given to those who had not overturned a load of corn in carrying at Harvest.

[3] Survives to this day as 'frummety'—wheat boiled in milk with cinnamon and sugar. From the Latin frumentum—wheat.—L. R. H.

CHAPTER 10

Who minds to quote
Upon this note,
May easily find enough;
What charge and pain,
To little gain,
Doth follow toiling plough.

Yet farmer may
Thank God and say,
For yearly such good hap;
Well fare the plough
That sends enow
To stop so many a gap.

TUSSER, 1557

A LOT of the best Corn land in Norfolk, land that was verry valuble in them days for corn growen is nothing now but a waste. I well rember a field at Narbrough a field that run to Nine Hundred Acre—for they have them big fields in that part of Norfolk. I have seen that field all under cultivation—now it is all growen up with Firs and thorns and no good to any man, and some of the best Barley land in Norfolk. That was the Farm I was Shepperd's page and sheep feeder on wen I was a lad.

Then there is another farm at East Walton, comprising one Thousand acres, in those days it was all under the plough and never a hedge on it, but now it is a verry diffrent story. The property of the Earl of Lester that was.

At last wen things were as bad as they could be, Joseph Arch come along
to be a Champion for Labour.[1] He told the Labour the truth—that they
were under fed, under paid, and under clothed. That must have been
about the year 1893.

He stood up in Norfolk and gathered the men round him, and told
them they must Orgernise. After a time they listened to him and see the
sence of what he said, and they did. Wages went up to fifteen shilling a
week and stayed there for a few years, and then they fell away from him
the man who had done it all. They thought that what he had done was
sure to go on—but did it? No. As soon as ever they droped the Orgernisa-
tion and the labour Club, all the trouble began again. Wages went down,
and Child Labour, and Woman Labour began.

Then Arch come again to there resque, but Farmers were stubben, and
some locked there men out, and on some Farms the men struck and things
got so that Norfolk was in a bad way. A lot of them nearly come to
starven, but work in the North of England was good, and hundreds of
young men took there famleys and went up there, and there they stayed,
and never saw there Native place again.

Things got better for a time but the Worken man is a stupid Animile
who never question any thing that hapen to him in them days, and they
let it drop and things got worse and worse for them. The Masters told the
men that Arch had left them and would trubble no more about them, but
it was not so,—the men had left Arch.

Arch spent his whole Life pleading the Worker's cause. It was he got
the Franchise for the Worker, but in them days voting was no secret, like

[1] Joseph Arch, born 1826 of labouring parents. He was self-educated and became in due
course a Methodist Preacher and a considerable master of oratory. He was a great upholder of
the rights of the working classes, and took their very real grievances greatly to heart. In 1872
he founded the National Agricultural Labourers' Union, and succeeded in obtaining a general rise
in wages and reform of various abuses. The rise in wages did literally destroy the Union, as the
men having gained this advantage lapsed from the Union. Arch was returned to Parliament as
member for West Norfolk in 1885, and was much respected in the House of Commons in spite
of his reputation as an 'Agitator' (that uncomfortable class of person so disliked by the mid-
Victorians) and his revolutionary ideas about a fair wage for the worker.—L. R. H.

it is today. The Master would go to the man and say, 'Wich way are you goen to vote John?' If the answer did not please him he would tell the man wich way he must vote, and John did it, or the Master made a spare man of him.

Most of the Labourers wore no colours, and did not know much better. Not so now, they mostly go there own road in politics.

I have seen Arch get up and make a speech on the green at my home, and the police would come along and move him on, or try to. They could not prosocute him, much as they would have liked to, and would if they could.

He was not like the man in Cornwall, Kellawny was his name, they put him in prison and said he was disturbing the pece of the Cuntry, but he stuck to the Cornish Miners till at last they sentenced him to Death. But the Cornish Miners got together and went to the town were he laid in Prison. They sang

> And shall Killawney die,
> If he do—
> Thirty thousand Cornish men
> Shall know the reason why—

But that was a great many years ago.[1]

After Arch had finished his work, then that grand old Man, Sir George Edwards took up the cause of the Norfolk Labour, and I am thankful to say carried it out to his death. His name and his memery will live for ever in the minds of the Working man. He knew the wants of the Worker, none better as he had been one of them himselfe.

In them days of fifty years ago there was no Employes Liabillity Act. If a neckleckfull farmer had delapadated carts and ladders and ropes, he had nothing to fear from the Law. Wen a man got hurt it was put down to accidents. He was Carted off to Hospital or the Poor House—his

[1] Sir Jonathan Trelawny, Bart., 1650-1721. He was created Bishop and imprisoned in 1688 for having opposed the Second Declaration of Indulgence by James the Second, having supported the first. The song refers to the Cornishmen's demonstration at his imprisonment, but it appears to have been of very short duration.—L. R. H.

children was alowed a little from the Parish,—his wife told to go out to work and keep them. If a Farmer's Bull gored a man they would say well he should not have gone near it—he knew the bull was dangerous; so there was no redress.

It did not matter either if the roof of his cottage let in the Rain, if he could not manage to repair it himself it had to go, and he and his must suffer.

All my life I have felt many and many a time, that the lot of the Farm Labourer has been harsher than any other Class of Workers. They were called evry sort of name—Jony Hodges, Clod hoppers, Louts, any other low term that come to there tongues, by the rest of the Workers and the Town People.

Well dear Reader as I have said I am not a religus man, but if you go back to earliest histry you will se there that the Bible tell us some thing about this. It says that the first tiller of the Earth was cursed by God. We find the two Brothers, Able and Cain. Able was a keeper of Sheep, and Cain a tiller of the ground. Both of those Brothers worked at there ocupations as was meant, and both Brothers ofered up a sacrifice to the Lord, no doubt to thank him for his goodness to them. The one brought the firstlings of his flock, and Cain the first fruits of the Earth.

We are not told what those fruits were that Cain ofered, or why God did not like them, but we are told that Cain's sacrifice was not axcepted by God. No wonder he was angry haven done his best, and he rose up and killed his Brother and became the first Murderer.

His Puniskment was severe, he was told that from hence forth the Earth should not bring forth her fullness, thorns and thissles should come up, and by the sweat of his brow he should eat bread. Beside that a mark was put upon him, and it seam to me as if the mark of Cain have been put upon the tiller of the Soil to this day, and the curse dwelt on the Earth.

But I think that the Tiller of the soil is the highest and oldest workman of all. No one can do without him and the product of his hands. The Gold miner canot eat his gold, nor the Coal miner his coal, nor the Iron miner

'By the sweat of thy brow shalt thou eat bread.'

his Iron. All and every one is dependent upon the tiller of the Soil. He is the Father of all Workers, like the old saying has it:

The King he governs all,
The Parson pray for all,
The Lawer plead for all,
The Ploughman pay for all
And feed all.

The Land is the Mother of all from beginning to end—as was promised —from dust thou came and to dust thou shalt return.

Well Lloyd George came along in due time, and a Liberill Government passed the Liabillity Act, the Free Edgeucation Act, and a law against children bein employed till they got to the age of forteen year.

I am glad to say that the children of Today have a lot better chance than they had forty or fifty year ago, wen they had to go to work at the age of eight or nine, or some times seven, but that does not mean I hold with this notion of longer years of edication we hear such a deal about these days.

How do they think that the Parents are goen to keep the Children to that age? Is the Government goen to find them food and clothes? I did not leave school a first class scoller, but I lernt enough to get my liven some how. But in them days Boys were Boys. Now you see them in the streets nothing but Babies, with a fag hangen on there lips.

All the same some People tell us that the world is much more enlightned now than then, so it is perhaps, but I am an old man and I think that in some things that enligtnment could well be despenced with. We have what they call Berth Controol, and any boy or girl can get books on such subjects, and others they had best be without to my thinken.

Well Lloyd George passed a greater Act still, the Old Age Pentcion Act. In the old time wen a man got too old to work, and there was none of there own folk as could or would help them, they had no choice, had'nt the old folk, but to live on some starvation alowence, or go to the poor House. Hundreds were druv from there homes to the Poor House were

they were parted for the rest of there lives. Men and women who had
been together always could not live together there, wich was cruel hard,
and against Nature.

Besides do not the Marrage laws say those two that God hath joined
together let no man put asunder.

CHAPTER II

THE DARK-EYED SAILOR

There was a comely young Lady fair
Who was walking out to take the air.
She met a Sailor by the way,
And I took notice of what they did say.

Said William, 'Dear Lady, why roam you alone,
The day is far gone and the night cometh on?'
She cried as the tears from her eyes they did fall,
''Tis my Dark-Eyed Sailor did prove my Downfall.

'It's seven long years since he left this land,
He took a gold ring from off my hand.
We broke the token. Here is half with me,
The other is rolling at the bottom of the sea.'

Said William, 'Drive him from your mind,
Some other Sailor as good you'll find.
Love turns aside and soon doth grow
Like the flowers of Spring under a mantle of snow.'

Those words did Mary's fond heart inflame,
She said, 'On me you shall play no game!'
She a pistol drew and then did cry,
'For my Dark-Eyed Sailor I'll live and die'.

Then half the ring did young William show.
She seemed distracted midst joy and woe,
Saying, 'Welcome William, I have lands and gold
For my Dark-Eyed Sailor true and bold'.

So maids be true and trusting while your love is far away,
For many a stormy morning brings forth a sunny day.

Obtained in MS. from the Author

CHAPTER 11

Give a thing—take a thing;
Never go to God again.

Traditional: South Norfolk

I THINK I have told enough of how things were at home to show I had no great fancy for the Jobs I might have had. They were no use to me—there was nothing else but the Old Game, and soon I was at it for all I was worth.

I had lerned how to make my owen nets, and I sone had plenty of them and a pair of Lurchers and I well knew how to use both. I rember once I was out one night and set a net at a gate, and sent my dogs to hunt the field. It turned out that there were a lot of lambs on it, which I did not know, and the dogs scattered them in all directions. One I am sorry to say ran at the gate and Broke its neck, which was unfortunate—but being done, me and my chum were rather pussled to know what to do with it, so he suggested we should take it away home to his house, which we did. We sckined it and Burried the skin the same night a mile from home. Strange to say that lamb was never missed, at least if it was we never herd of it.

The rearin season soon came round again, and I got to know that they had reared a large number of tame Partridges not far from my place. There was a chance for me, and with a little spyen and some enquirs I sone made out were they were feeden. The night befor they came into season, my mate and me took the net and dragged a large medaw and caught one hundred and sixty, I believe it was. Of corse they were missed and they came to me straight away, but the birds were in Norwich by that time, and so I had the laugh of them again.

The Partridge netter is the greatest enemy the Keeper have. If the season start dark he is after the birds as sone as the corn is cut, but if the Keeper get there first with his Busshes,[1] that completly spoil the Poacher's game. His net is sone tangled up, but it is not often that he is caught like that, as either the Poacher or his scouts know where the Busshes are. The Partridge like to sit were he can see any thing comen—on Barly stubbles or big medaws, as he know he have many enimies, the netter, the cat, the fox, the stoat, and the rat. All those animals are night workers and are keen hunters after there prey, but the netter is the most deadly of them all.

I used to get a lot of Phesants with the Partriges, as the Phesants do not go up to the trees to roost before they have got over there first moult, but stop on the ground for warmth. Of cors they are as good as the Partriges as the dealers hang them in the ice safe till the time comes in for them to sell. Years ago there used to be a good sale for Live Birds, but that seem to have died out, like a lot of other things that have changed with the years.

Well, I caried the Game on for a year or two with a lot of sucess. I dare say it cost me some thing like 40£ in fines, but that did not matter to me as I was enjoyen myself to my hart's content. I did not mind payen there fines as long as I kept my Liberty. Some times the Maderstrates rubbed it in pretty hot for me, and I got a pretty good name, but I gloried in that. Also I got my own back some times and brought a hornet's nest about the ears of a lot of the people in the village I lived in who were agin me one way and another. It happened this way.

The Parish were I was born had, as I have told befor, a great lot of Comon land enclosed. The money for the rents of those Comons was suposed to go to the Parishners in the shape of Coals at Christmas time, but evry year it kept getten lower and lower. It happened one day tha` a frend of mine came across the Histry of the Charities of Norfolk in a verry old book. I had a look at it and found by that book there were a lot of things to do with the villige lands and monies that the People did

---

[1] Thorn bushes cut and stuck over the fields to entangle the nets.

not know about or had forgot. As I have said the People of the seventies and the fore part of the eighties were verry ignorent, and the Upper classes led them were they liked. In that way a lot of the old rights and customs had died out.

Well, after I had got hold of that book and found out what I did, it did not take me long to get a lot of the People together and tell them of these things which I thought they should know. Some would say 'I have heard my father talk about them things'. The Comons used to bring in a matter of fifty Pounds a year as the great Eastern Railway cut through the Comons and paid twenty five pounds a year for that ground.

The Parson used to give out some times that there would be a Parish meeting held in the Vestry of the Church at eleven o'clock fore noon. Well I, not caren who I ofended, got some of the younger men who were house holders, to go with me and see the Parson and the other Oficials, and ask to have this meeting held at night, so that all the Parishoners could attend. They had to do this, and when it came to the night there was a Lawyer and the Gentleman Farmers and a lot of others there. They had begun to think that there was something brewing and had got in Policeman to keep order in case there was a row.

The meeting was held in a Barn, and they started off by asking us what it was we wanted. I had an Endipindent Gentleman at my back, and the shop keepers and some small tradesmen and all the Parish. Some one sugested there should be a Cheer man, and I was elected. I told the Gentlemen what this meeting was Called for—we wanted to know were those lost Charyties were gone to and what had become of the money.

The Lawyer he got up and wanted to know what I knew about lost Charyties, so I shewed him my book, and read out of it to all the meeting what was due to the Parish of Pentney from the lands that had been left to them in the old days, by them that was dead and gone.

The Lawyer wanted to tell us that all those things had been dropt so ong that they could not be brought back again, but I had him there all ight. There was a lady lived in the Parish the early part of the Eighteenth

Century, and she built four Cottages on some waste land. The rents of these cottages were left to the Parish to provide so much bread to each house, and a half crown to every Widow, to be distributed on St. Thomas morning in every year. All this had died out and I wanted to know where those rents had gone to. The Gentleman farmer colected them that I did know, but he did not seem to want to tell me what he did with the money. When he was pressed to tell he said he took the monies to the Church.

There was also a plot of land which had been left to the Parish for ever, so that the income from it might bind two of the children from the bigest families in the villige to a trade as aprentices. The Lawyer had been doing all the talking for the others, and now he asked me if I knew were this piece of land was situated, thinking to catch me that way. I told him I did and pointed it out to him.

Besides all these there was another twelve Acres of land, the rent of which had been left to be distributed to the poor, in the shape of Blankets and other wares to be given at Christmas time. As it happened acording to the bequest, they should have been distributed at this same Gentleman farmer's house. The Farm belonged to a Lady by the name of Thackery (were this Gentleman lived) and was called Ashwood Lodge. I believe his Grandfather and Father had farmed the land before him, but now I believe the family have all died out. Of corse he knew all about them things—the Gentleman farmer I mean, but it suted him not to say too much. Dumb as a Mawkin (Scarecrow) he were.

Of corse the Lawyer blustered and thretned and all that, and said he would have the Poor Law Comisners down and that if they did come the Parish would have to pay for them. Be that as it may, the next year wen the time came round, the Dole Cole came to a ton, and the Blankets and all the other things were given to the verry old people in the villige as had been meant by those as had left the money.

I had almost forgotten to say that beside these matters there were three Alms Houses in the Parish which had got verry much out of repair and were hardly fit for human habitation. They took the money from the piece of land that I have mentioned and repaired those Alms Houses which had been a crying need for longer than enough.

Do not think dear Reader that I got a lot of credit for taken this Job in hand. As some of the older worken men in the villige said to me—the trouble was I knew too much. One thing is certain that if the Parson and the Lawyer and some more besides who thought as they did, could have killed me by looks I should sone have been dead, but I did not care for any of them. Even some of the other Parishners tried to do me all the harm they could after that, even though they never knew nothing of those lost Charyties, none but the verry old people in the villige could rember any thing of them. Neither should I have known but for the book, and it comen into my hands by chance, which was a bit of good luck for some.

Bein an outlaw in the eyes of some of them, what they thought did not trubble me, but it seems as I had trubbled them, and they wanted to be rid of me. Any how a few weeks after all this had hapened I got a letter one day to tell me that they would get me a free Passage to Canidia if I would like to go. But I was not to be driven out of my Cuntry by any of them, I was always ready to take what they could do for me but not to be coersed by them, that did not sute me at all.

.   .   .   .   .

Perhaps some as reads this will think as I am against all Parsons and Church and Religon, but that is not so. I am not a religous man by a long way, but I do not dispise religon, though we canot pick up a paper but what we see some Devlish things done under its name. I have studded the Bible a lot in my time, but like many more can never onderstand it all. It tell us what to do and what not to do—and one cannot help but see if people do even a bit as it tells us this World would be a much better place. I am not goen to say that there are not some good People to day—as good as there ever were, but they are hard to find. It seam to me that religon is mostly money.

There are a lot of People try to get to Heaven by diffrent ways. There are many kinds of religon in England to-day—it always seam to me like three men meeting at Cross Roads. There is a Sign Post standing there with the words on—'To London'. One Man says 'That is the way we want to go, that is the direction post to London'. Another one say, 'No, this is the road'. The last one say, 'No, this is the road'. They all want to get to London but by diffrent roads. It is the same way with the diffrent classes of religon, they all want to get to Heaven but by diffrent ways and means. I think that from time imorell religon has been one of the crulest and blodiest things that the world have known, from the earliest Martires to the present day.

Party feeling and religon have caused more wars and blood shed than anything I know of. Take Ireland to day—Se the murders that have been done there with the diffrent coads of religon. It is said that God made Soloman the wisest man that ever lived. I wonder if God gave sence and Wisdom to men so that they might make Poison Gasses and mashine guns and all sorts of Weppons to kill there felow men. Still we must rember the Bible tells us that there will be wars and rumers of wars, but the time will come wen men will beat there spears to pruning hooks and there swords into plow shears, and learn war no more—but as long as the present state of religon exsist that time will never come.

I was reading some time ago of two farmers, that owned each a pice of land, on the opisite side of the road. They met one day to plant there fields, one was a verry religous man, the other a verry Worldly man. The religous man said, 'I hope we shall both have good crops Nebour'. 'Yes,' said the Worldly man, 'I hope so.' 'I will pray that we may', said the Religious man. Well, the season went on and the wheat which they had planted grew and so did the weeds; the religous man kept on with his prears, but the Worldly man sent his Labours to cut the weeds away from his crops. At harvest they met again. The Worldly man had a good crop, the Religous man a good crop of weeds. 'But', said the Religous man, 'I praid for a good crop—I suppose the Lord did not think fit that I should have one.' 'Ah,' said the Worldly man, 'you let your hoe rust in your hand—the Lord helps them that help themselves.'

There is a deal of truth in that story.

Well, my frends, we have a verry few John Wesleys and Robert Rakes in our Pulpits to day. I can well rember wen the old-fashoned Labour preacher would walk ten or twelve miles on a Sunday to preach. They did not ask for pay, they were the men who practiced what they preched. To day most of them preach one thing and practice another, some thing like the Parson's creed

> Money, O money thy praises I sing,
> Thou art my Saviour, my Lord and my King,
> It is for thee that I preach, for thee that I pray,
> And give praises to God three times in the day.

CHAPTER 12

INFALLIBLE SIGNS OF RAINY WEATHER

DEDUCED FROM OBSERVATIONS OF DIVERS ANIMALS

If Ducks and Drakes their Wings do flutter high,
Or tender Colts upon their Backs do lye;
If Sheep do bleat, or play, or skip about,
Or Swine hide Straw by bearing on their Snout;
If Oxen lick themselves against the Hair,
Or grazing Kine to feed apace appear,
If Cattle bellow, gazing from below,
Or if Dog's Entrails rumble to and fro;
If Doves or Pigeons in the Evening come
Later than usual to their Dove house home;
If Crows and Daws do oft themselves be-wet
Or Ants and Pismires home apace do get;
If in the Dust Hens do their Pinions shake,
Or by their flocking a great Number make;
If Swallows fly upon the Water low,
Or Wood-Lice seem in Armies for to go;
If Flies, or Gnats, or Fleas infest and bite,
Or sting more than they're wont by Day or Night;
If Toads hie Home, or Frogs do croak amain,
Or Peacocks cry:—Soon after look for Rain.

The New Book of Knowledge, 1758

CHAPTER 12

Thus I live
But rather guess for quietness
As others do, so do I too.
Content me here
To live upright

TUSSER, 1557

ABOUT this time a strange thing hapened, at least, considring how I got my living and the name I had, it was a strange thing to hapen to me. A Gentleman came down to Norfolk and bought an estate close to where I lived. It seam that the Farmers told him about me, and one day he sent for me to go and se him. Well I went and wen I got there what should he do but offer me the place of Game Keeper.

I dont say that I was not surprised, but there it was, and I thought to myself, just the Job for me. I had verry little knolidge of the work, but I was determined to do my best as the Job apeled to me, so I agreed to take the place and went to that Gentleman on a month's liken [liking, approval]. I stayed with him ten years, and gave him Satisfaction, as the Boys knew me, and so they never trubbled me. They wold work on the outside of my ground but they left me alone, and the result was I always had plenty of game.

I had a good Master. He used to say to me if you are honest and good to your trust I will be honest to you.

There was a lot of People that used to sneer at me in my new Job, and some of them took the trubble to sit down and rite to my Master telling him what my past life had been like. He had one answer for them all which they got no change out of. He used to say, 'I took my Game keeper

on without a refernce, and I am quite prepared to find out what he is
like myself'.

Well, I sone found that the life of a Keeper is not all honey, not by a
long way. He have to put up with a lot of Jeers and Grins as he go along,
and a lot of grivences from some people. On the other hand it is a verry
intresting life for the man that will study nature, as well as see to his
Keepering. He will sone find out a lot of things that a man will never
know if he goes about with his gun ready to kill anything that moves in
the shape of vermin as so many do.

For instance, if he sees a stoat or weasell carrien a mouse or young
rabbitt; if he use a little sence he may track it to its young ones and get
the lot. Both the stoat and weasell are bold and fearless and pay little
atention to a man if he is quiet. Also if they have young to feed they will
nearly always come back to there prey if they have been forced to drop it.

The same in the summer time wen the horks are nesting. If the keeper
sees a hork strike a bird and carry it away, not just fly to a tree to strip and
eat it, if he follow the direction he may often come on the nest. The young
horks make a hissing and screaming that can be heard a long way, and if
the Keeper destroy the brood they are not left to starve. Many keepers
shoot on sight and do not care about the young. I do not pretend to be any
more kindhearted than other men, but I belive in being as human as
posible to Animals and birds.

As I have said befor it is an intresting life. I have always been verry fond
of dogs so I took a great delight in training them for shooting. I trained a
great many for one Gentleman living at Saffen Walden. He was my
Master's Lawer, and got me a lot of dogs to train. It is a long Job and
takes a rare lot of Patence, but of corse some are much easier than others.
Like humans some have a lot more sence than others, but I was posesed of
plenty of Patence, and with that and kindness I mostly managed it. I had
only one that I could not learn everything I wanted him to do. Some are
born teachable, some are verry stubben—they are the worst to train and
come in most for the whip.

If you have a stubben one try him first with kindness. If that fail you, and its not often that it does, you must try Punishment, but kindness mostly win in the end.

I do not think there is a more sencible dog than the old English curly coted Retrever, though you dont see many of them about these days. It is hard to beat him as a sporting dog. I have trained a lot of Spanells, but they are a class of dog that if you get one that will do as he is told you will get others that are verry wilfull.

On the estate we had a large wood full of scotch firs, and there were always large numbers of Wood Pigons in it. My plan wen I started training a young dog, was to watch and find were the Pigons fed. Then I made a hide under a tree—you must go softly as there is no bird so quick and wary, or so hard to shoot except perhaps the Jay. Wen I had shot a Pigon I used to keep the dog in till I told him to fetch it. Of corse first he must be taught to retreve, which was done with a stuffed Pigon skin.

By August the Plover and Duck came in season, and as we had a lot of marsh and fen land on the estate, I could let the dog follow me there, and tell him to stand till I told him to seek the Dead, and got to be able to depend on him to be steady.

I had one retrever bitch that would find Plover's eggs and bring them two at a time in her mouth without cracking them. It was she who once saved my life.

I was out after duck one verry sharp night in winter. I shot one and the bitch Jumped a fairly large dyke to fetch it. Wen she started to come back with the duck she tried to walk over the ice and wen she was well out in the middle it broke and let her in. She could not get a foothold, and was like to go under the ice, so I got down to the edge to help her and the side gave way and there I was up to my neck in freezing mud and water and stuck fast.

As luck would have it the bitch got out some how and came down the bank to me and I got hold of her collar, and by clinging to that and a little bit of a bush I strugled out. If she had not been there I must have smotherd, but as it was I never took any harm and was soon home, but am thinking I am payen a lot of price for them duckings now I am old.

You may be shure I thought a lot of her after that, but like evry thing we human beings set the most store by, some thing is shure to happen to them. I was out shooting with my Master and a Gentleman and he wounded a hare by the side of the Railway. The hare got on the line and my bitch went to fetch it. Just at that moment a train came, ran over her and of corse killed her.

I felt the loss of her as much as I would of a frend, I could never get her equall for sagasity and sence.

Well, my life as a Keeper was like many other things, I had to put up with a lot some times. My plan if I found the men were putting snares about as they often would, was to stay by them till the man come to take them up, and then tell him if I caught him any more I should report him and that mostly finished that trubble.

I beleve in barkin befor biten.

I always found that the men on the farms would give there mates away sooner than any one else. I turned a deaf ear to there tales, and told them I would find out all I wanted to know for myself, and did not give them any thanks for there information. They soon found they could not curry faveaur with me. I knew well enough they would as soon have given me away if they got the chance, haven been there befor so to speak.

I consider the farmer is about the bigest enimy the keeper have. If you once get rong with him you are for it, as he is always about and can do you a lot of harm. He can put his foot on a nest of eggs and no one be the wiser. A sheeperd can be a great hinderence to a keeper to as he is always about with his sheep. In fact the Keeper have to mind and not fall out

vith any one of them. Of corse the Labour is were you can always find
im, and he is careful not to get rong with the keeper if he can help it,
s it does him no good.

I well rember my first case up at Grimstone Petty Sessions, as in the past
had been me that had been the other side of the dock so to speak. It was
case of Poaching, and the man was a chap that used to think he could
o as he liked with me, only he found out his mistake. I had warned him
any a time, and he would give me some verry insulting langage, till at
st I was forced to sumon him.

Wen the case was called on of corse my name was called as Prosacuter.
ir W. Bagg was in the Chair, and he looked at me as of corse I had been
vell known there but not quite in the same Position I ocupyed that day.
hen he asked me if I was the man that had been befor them many times.
told him I was. 'Well,' he said, 'Its a long lane that never turns'; and
vith that he wished me the best of luck. I know in those days my Master
vas often asked how I was behaven myself.

My work was not wholy Keeperen. My Lady found out that I was
andy and could do a lot of Jobs, so wen there was any Pictures to be
ung, or Carpetts streched I was always called in.

She was an Australian Lady—took some pleasen some times, had been
sed to Black servants I suppose which made her so severe perhaps. I
lways managed to get on well with her, as she had one son, a weakly
3oy about sixteen years old. He could not do the things most boys do, and
t often fell to my lot to amuse him.

The days that he could manage to get out I used to tell him about the
hings that I thought would intrest him. If I found a rare bird's nest such
s the nest of the Crested Ren or long tailed Tit Mouse. I would show him
hat. So I got on well with his Mother. The Master was not his father as
he Lady had been married twice.

I never got into any serious trubble keepering but once. A cupple of
oung men had stolen a gun and started to poach with it. I sone got the
ews of what was hapening and wen I was out one night soon after I herd

the report of a gun from a wood near by. I went to the wood and hi
behind some holly Busshes, and they walked right out onto the top of m
Of corse I told them that I should report it, and the one with the gun can
at me with it clubbed and struck at my head. Had he caught my head I
would have brained me, but he hit my shoulder, discollating it. I neve
felt it at the time, it hapened to be the left one, and I struck him on th
head with my stick and knocked him sencless.

The other man had had enough and run away and left his pall, but as
knew him that did not matter.

Wen the first man came round with a verry sore head he cried an
wanted to be forgiven, and I have no doubt it was the excitement of bei
caught that made him try and brain me. I let him go home as by then m
shoulder was giving me great pain.

The next morning I went and told my Master what had hapened an
he at once drove me to Lynn Hospetlle were they put my shoulder righ
The two lads were arested the same day. I had the gun and wen the Polic
came to me they at once reconized it as the stolen one.

The lad that had struck me got six months and the other three month
and then they were both Charged with stealing the gun, and got a furth
term of Prison for that. Wen they came out my Master did all he cou
for them. He found Employment on the place for the one that struck m
and the other man went to a Job in London, but was killed in a sew
there. The other had had quite enough of Poaching, settled down, g
married and became an honest man. Many times he have told me
was the best day's work he ever done, as the Emprisonment made a ma
of him.

After that I had not much bother as the older men had some respect f
me and would not trubble me—besides a half gallon of beer went a lor
way with some of them, and as time went on I could go any where ar
not get insulted as I had been at the start.

One thing I might menction which I verry soon lerned both from bein
a Poacher and haven to do with them as a Keeper. If there is a big Sho

I struck him on the head with my stick.

goen on, and the Poacher come along and ask for a day's beating, and he is told, 'No, you are a Poacher' it is a great mistake on the Head Keeper's part.

It is this way. If the poacher is beating with the others the keeper know verry well were he is, but if on the other hand the poacher is followen up the Guns, he is looking after himself and making his bag all right. There are alwys a lot of game comen back wounded, and he is spoting them. So he go on all day behind the guns, and pick up all he can find. It pay the keeper to have him onder his eye.

Wen I was Keepering I used to get all the Poachers I knew of to beat for me, as then I knew were they were. Besides the Poacher say—'Old so and so is not a bad sort, he alway give us a Job wen he can', and for that reason they will be more likely to leave him alone. There is a lot of ways they can get at you as well as Poaching.

I well rember a Farmer near me who had got rong with some chaps. He had a splendid tree of Peaches on the wall onder his bed room window. He was a lot set on those peaches and used to rake the gravel pathes onder neath to se if any one come near the tree to interfer with them.

Of corse they were spotted by a cupple of the Boys, and a sale found for them. Wen the Farmer got up one fine morning he found the tree stripped and the Peaches gone and never a foot mark left on the raked gravel—they might have flown away.

Of corse the Police were called in to find them but I expect they were eat befor he had done looken for them, any how those two Boys were never found out.

I think it was that same Policeman, and a verry clever man he was, who was told that there were some Ducks stolen, and he was soon on the Job. He went about verry bussy serching for those stolen ducks, and the Boys vent and stole his own, and that was the last he ever saw of them, he never found any thing of them again.

As I said befor I had a good Master, he gave me evry opportunity to njoy my Job, always took out a two pound licence for me to kill out layen game, and considered me evry way. Many and many a time he would come down and say 'Get your gun man and we will have a prowl round'. Looken back I see that was the happiest ten years I have ever knowen, but like all good things which befall Humanity it come to a finish. My Master had some sort of trubble and had to sell the place and go away. It meant bad luck for me to as I was throwen out of my Job, and sorry I was for it.

If he is alive now he is geten an old man like myself, but it is many a year since I have heard of him. They wrote to me from some place in Scotland and told me the Boy had died there, but then he was always ailing, poor lad.

CHAPTER 13

THE CONDITION OF MAN

Naturally a Man is hairy as the Lion
Strong and Worthy as the Ox
Large and Liberal as the Cock
Avaricious as the Dog
Hardy and Swift as the Hart
Debonair and True as the Turtle Dove
Malicious as the Leopard
Gentle and Tame as the Dove
Crafty and Guilful as the Fox
Simple and Mild as the Lamb
Shrewd as the Ape
Light as the Horse
Soft and Pitiful as the Bear
Dear and Precious as the Elephant
Good and Wholesome as the Unicorn
Vile and Slothful as the Ass
Fair and Proud as the Peacock
Gluttonous as the Wolf
Envious as the Bitch
Rebel and Inobedient as the Nightingale
Humble as the Pigeon
Fell and Foolish as the Ostrich
Provident as the Pismire
Dissolute and Vagabond as the Goat
Spiteful as the Pheasant
Soft and Meek as the Chicken
Moveable and Varying as the Fish
Letcherous as the Boar
Strong and Puissant as the Camel
Traiterous as a Mule
Advised as a Mouse
Reasonable as an Angel.

And therefore he is called the LITTLE WORLD, or else he is
called ALL CREATURES, for he doth take Part of ALL.

The New Book of Knowledge, 1758

CHAPTER 13

They wanted us to go to school
And to turn the pages of books
Why learn the language of books
When the forest speaks to you?
One cannot eat books,
And pens and pencils are poor weapons
To kill the deer of the mountains
And the grunting boar.

ANON.

A KEEPER gets to know a lot about the life that goes on round him if he keep his eyes open as I have said before, and what with Poaching and Keepering, and bein always fond of liven things, I think I got to know more than most.

Take the Rany or shrew. I saw some were that a lot of People wondred why at some times of year they saw so many layen dead by the roads and hedges. One day I was sitten quiet under a hedge, and I herd some squeeling going on in the Grass. Presently two shrews came right up to my feet and fought a battle, or rather a wresling match, as they were both trying to grip the other in there fore legs. At length one succeeded and simply hugged the other to death. They are terrible little fighters and many of them get killed.

Then I have been asked by John Knowlittle,[1] 'Did the viper really swallow her young in time of danger?' I told him no, as I had frequently seen the young ones layen beside the mother no longer than needles, and

[1] Pen name of Mr. A. H. Patterson, the naturalist and author.

I have seen them slip into the grass in time of danger and come out again. At any alarm the mother give a hiss, and the young run all over her to hide or get to the grass or moss, or any cover that's nearest. It may seam as if she swallowed them, but its not true like a lot more cuntry tales.

The same way they say that a Hedgehog will suck cows—I am well aware he is verry fond of milk, but that is an impossible thing for him to do, as even if his mouth was big enough his teeth are so placed that he would bite the cow's teats, and she would emidegetly get up and walk away. The Hedgehog is a verry distructive animile amongst game. If he find a Partridge nest he will eat all the eggs, and any thing else he can get, toads, frogs and young birds, and any sort of flesh. If put to it he is a vegetairan as well, and will even eat crab apples, when he can find them. I have dug out half a peck of crabbs from rabbitt burries and other holes were he have laid them up for the winter.

The Hedgehog is easily caught in a box trap, baited with a pice of fish, or a terrier will find them wen they are out hunting for food on parks and medaws. They say they are verry good eaten, at least the Gypsys find them so.

We were not much troubled with Gypsys were I was Keeper as we were some distance from the main road, but some used to camp on a comon about half a mile from my house. The old Lady used to gadabout with a basket selling tapes and cottons and other small things. One day she come to my door and there was a hedgehog layen on the bench. She wanted to know what I was goen to do with it—would I give it to her? I wanted to know what she was goen to do with it, and she said eat it.

After that she alwys called to see if I had one for her, and later on she showed me how they cooked the thing. They removed the inside, wrapt the Hedgehog Bristless and all in clay, piled a fire on the clay, lit it, and let it bake. Wen she thought it had done enough, she took it out and cracked off the clay, and the bristless came off with it. She did not get me to taste it, but it looked all rite and the smell seam good.

She was a good old Body, and learnt me lots of little things in the docterine line. Her name was Greay, one of the oldest Gypsy names, so I have been told.

The Hedgehog will kill and eat snakes of which there are plenty in Norfolk—grass snakes and Vipers, but I have never seen a Viper in Suffolk. The cattle used to get bitten by the viper, genrilly on the chin wen they were feeding, but if taken in time the poison is easly killed with salt, but if the bite is not looked to the animile die. The grass snake is easley known by the yellow rim round his neck. They are no trubble to tame and make intrestin pets. We had two in a glass box for a long time, and used to feed them on small birds and raw meat, but they will lie dorman all the winter unless you keep them very warm. I never saw them atempt to bite, but they will rear up and hiss and pretend to strike, which they cannot do as they have no fangs.[1]

Most dogs hate snakes and some will get them by the back of the neck and bite them so they are paralised and cannot shut there mouths, some trick they must know by instinct. The grass snake is as much at home in the water as he is on land, and goes riggling along like an eel and just as fast.

The slow Worm is perfectly harmless to, but he is hardly a snake. Crows and other Birds of Pray will kill and eat them if they get a chance.

Three animiles that trubble the keeper a lot are the stoat, the weasell and the miniver. They are all of a class—they kill for the sport of killing verry often more than for hunger. The stoat is not verry big but he is so blood-thirsty he will kill any thing he can master. The mother stoat bring out her young about the month of May, four to six in a litter—she genrelly find a nice dry stub that is hollow for her nest. As sone as the

[1] Some might like to try the following method of 'charming' a grass snake, which I have seen and found work,—but I have not tried it on a poisonous one!

Hold the snake lightly head downwards, letting it slip quietly from hand to hand as if you were going to let it slide to the ground, but as it slips through the hand, put the back hand rapidly to the front, so that it is continuously slipping head downwards through one's half-closed palms. The snake will gradually grow less and less lively, and when it is quiet coil it in the palm of one hand with the head resting up the arm towards the crook of the elbow. Breathe on it several times and cover it lightly with your other hand cupped for a moment or two. When you remove your hand the snake will lie perfectly motionless until purposely disturbed.—L. R. H.

young ones can run well they go hunting with the old one, I have seen them running and hunting like a pack of hounds. If you can kill the mother the young ones are easy to get as they will not leave the old one.

Wen the stoat get onto a rabbitt, they never leave it till they have killed it, no matter were the rabbit go, unless by chance they lose the scent, the stoat folow till the rabbit lay down and is killed. Such a fear does a rabbitt have of them that it will run quite slowly almost to your feet and never notice, it seems as if its wits and its strength are both gone.

All the stoat tribe are great destroyers of game and game eggs. A hen Phesant with a brood of young will drive a stoat off by fighting him, but he will mostly have one of her young ones befor he go.

I have seen them bring a squirell down from a tree as they are good Climers. A stoat will climb and kill the young of the Wood Pigon, throw them down the tree and take them to there young. I have also seen a stoat carry a young rabbitt from the nest slung across her shoulder when she found it was to big and heavy to take any other way. Wen I moved she dropped it and I found it was alive not being bitten at the back of the neck and sucked which is the way stoats kill rabbitts, but through the base of the spine so it was paralised and could not struggle. Stoats have not much fear of man if he stay quiet, and will come back to fetch prey they have been forced to drop.[1]

The one useful thing they do is to destroy rats, making there home in stacks and killing the rats as long as there are any left. I once saw a stoat catch a full grown hare. The hare tried evry way to shake the stoat off, and I had to shoot both of them. If they can get into a coop of young fowles they will kill evrey one and perhaps carry none away, nor ever come back to that place again.

Well I might keep on riten for ever about the stoat, as I do not think you could lern all his ways in a life time. In some seasons he will change his coat to White, all except the black tuft on the end of his tail. I have

---

[1] Stoats like shrews are great fighters, and I have found them lying dead in the same way as the shrews after a particularly fierce battle.—L. R. H.

killed some of them verry prettley marked with brown and white. They are easley trapped in boxes lett through a bank at the corners of woods, if the trap is set so they can se the light they are sure to run through.

Next we have the Weasell second cousin to the stoat but smaller. He is how ever just as vicious. I have seen them kill a full grown rabbitt many a time. I always found that the best way to get them was to fill an egg with strichnine, as they are verry fond of eggs. You will not often catch them in a trap as they are so light they will not easily spring a steel trap.

Weasells will get into a Partridge's nest and eat evry egg as well as killing any young ones. The female is verry curagous and determend when she has young. I once saw a litter of young ones go in a hole so I set a small trap and caught one of the young ones in it. I hung it up above the trap and got the mother, and she kept tryen to Jump to the young one while she was in the trap.

Then there is the mouse Hunter or Miniver. I dont think they kill anything except mice and frogs. You can easly tell the Weasell from the Miniver because the Weasell have wiskers and the Miniver none for all that some people say they are the same.

Evry one is familer with the ferritt, and verry useful he is but just as bad if he run lose, as like them he is never tired of killing for the sake of killing. I never saw only one Polecat in Norfolk, although they are plentifull in Linconshire they seldom seam to reach Norfolk.

I think the Fox and the domestic Cat are the worst of all the Keeper's enimies, as they both take the old Bird off her nest and all the clutch is spoilt. As to the Fox you can gaurd against his deperadations with a few worn out traps or old hoops. They will keep him away from a nest as he is a cuning chap, and is not goen to put his foot into danger if he knows it.

I have often seen a nest ready to hatch at night and the next morning
they have all been killed and the eggs spoilt. A siting bird loses her scent
to a great extent, but they always keep moving about there eggs Just
before they Hatch, and the scent seam to come on them again and then
the Fox get them.

The Cat is nearly as bad at this game but as sone as the Keeper spo
his footing a trap is set for him with a pice of rabbitt as a bait, and you are
pretty sure to have him. True there is a law against bating traps for Cats,
but laws like Promises are made to be broken wen there is a Job on hand.

The Hawk is another enimy of the Keeper. He will swoop down on
a covey of Birds and take one in a moment. All sort of hawks are alike
in this—there is the Kestrill and the Henharrier and the Merlin, but he
mostly enhabitt the north. Where I was Keeper we had a large rabbitt
warren and we shot three or four Goshawks wile I was there. I have seen
one of those hawks pick up a half grown rabbitt and fly away with it
easly, but it is not verry often you see them.

The Kestrill will pounce on young Phesents and take them from a
coop on the rearing ground, and they are so quick and silent they may
get sevrell before the Keeper get a shot at them.

The Torney Owl will get young Birds in the woods, as he often prowl
about in the daytime, still he kill a lot of Weasells and rats so what harm
he do the Keeper in one way he make up in a nother way.

Some years ago there was a lot of talk about the Eleuminated Owl in
Norfolk. Many of the older people will rember it as the news papers
were full of it for sevrell weeks. John Knowlittle had a lot to say about it
and a nother Gentleman from Warham took a lot of intrest,—I think his
name was Birch. Any way I rote to him and told him of an experence
I had wen a boy. I went to a hollow tree one night for some young
Jackdaws, and wen I pulled my arm out of the hole it was covered with
a kind of light wich I have since found to be Phosferus, such as the Glow
worm and the fire flie carry. As I told him I had no doubt but what the
Owl had been liven in one of them hollow trees, and that accounted for

the glow on the fethers. Of corse there was a lot of exadgeration on the subject, and all sorts of tales about, but as I have found befor if you look far enough you can nearly always find a reason for most things.

I got into comunation with that Gentleman and found he was a bit of a Natulist and informed him on many points.

The Jay is an Egg eater like the Hoddie crow and both are waged war upon by the keeper, as you will see if you happen to go through a wood were the Keeper's Gallows tree is hung out.[1] You will find nearly evry kind of vermin there except the fox and that chap he is suposed to let severly alone. But there comes a time wen if they get to numerus they must be checked, and then its done one way or another.

Some places in Norfolk wen the Keeper find a litter of cubs he send to the master of the Hounds, and they come and dig them out and take them away. By that means he do not have so much bother with them.

Wen a Keeper have a trout river or lake to look over he come up against another sort of enimy—the Otter, as they will destroy a lot of fish. They are another animile which is easly trapped wen you find were they have been working. I have Poisned them with a large Eel by putting some strichnine in a slit in the eel's back and layen it in some shallow water. If you know were they are, which you may do by finding the tracks they make on leavin the water and the broad mark of there tails, you may often shoot them as they swim up stream.

The Fishing Acosation at Lynn used to pay me two and six for every otter's foot and the same for the Herons. I rember being out one night after dark, and an Otter swam up to me with four young ones. I shot the old one and the young ones kept swimming round and round, and I killed the lot of them.

There was a Water Weel on the Nar, to work a pump to carry the water from the Marshes, with a sluce door to hold the river water up, to work the water weel. Wich ever way the otter came he had to leave

[1] I remember as a child counting no less than thirteen enormous cats hanging in one of these 'larders' well hidden (perhaps luckily) in the depths of a large wood.—L. R. H.

the water there, and I trapped a great many at that spot. With a large
trap and a strong chain they are soon drowned.

The Heron fall an easy prey to the man looking after fish. The way to
get him is to get a fish hook and put a live roach on it, like baiting a
hook for pike. Lay the bate in a shallow place, give the Heron enough
line to let him get on the bank, and you will find him there as the Heron
never eat what he catch in the water. I have seen them kill water rats
and take them out to eat on the bank.

You may some times come on them and shoot them wich is the better
way, but it is not verry often you can do it, as the Heron can se a long
way and is always on the alirt for danger.

I lerned a lot from nature. It taught me to think at an early age, and
I have tried to studdy her in all her secerets, but there is a lot I could
never lern. I have lerned the way of Birds and Animiles and Insects, and
a lot I have lerned in the ways of men as well, as with both of them it
comes from keepen quiet and watching.

I have herd lots of men call themselves honest men and perhaps most
People thought they were, but by watching I have found that they, like
others, were honest till found out.

There are a lot of People have a good charcter in the Day light that
would not be verry bright in the dark if they could be seen. For my part
I would much rather trust the man that did not pretend to be so honest,
than I would the selfe honest man. Mostly
they are men that shake you by the hand
and stick a knife in you at the same time.

I have seen men that atended the Church
and Chapel regular, any one would think
that they were so honest they could not
go rong if they tried. I think Christ was
quite right wen he said beaware of them
that come to you in sheep's Clothing—
for they are inward raving Wolves.

CHAPTER 14

THE FAKENHAM GHOST

Benighted was an ancient dame,
And fearful haste she made
To gain the vale of Fakenham,
And hail its willow shade.

Her footsteps knew no idle stops,
But followed faster still;
And echo'd to the darksome copse
That whispered on the hill.

Darker it grew, and darker fears
Came o'er her troubled mind;
When now, a short quick step she hears
Come patting close behind.

She turned; it stopt! naught could she see
Upon the gloomy plain!
But as she strove the Sprite to flee,
She heard the same again.

Yet once again amidst her fright,
She tried what sight could do;
When through the cheating glooms of night—
A Monster stood in view!

On she sped and hope grew strong,
The white park gate in view;
Which pushing hard—so long it swung,
That Ghost and all passed through.

Loud fell the gate against the post!
Her heart strings like to crack:
For much she feared the grisly ghost
Would leap upon her back.

Still on, pat, pat, the Goblin went,
As it had done before—
Her strength and resolution spent,
She fainted at the door.

Out came her husband much surprised,
Out came her daughter dear;
Good natured souls! All unadvised
Of what they had to fear.

The candle's gleam pierced through the night,
Some short space o'er the green;
And there the little trotting sprite
Distinctly might be seen.

An Ass's Foal had lost its dam
Within the spacious park;
And simple as the playful lamb
Had followed in the dark.

No Goblin he; no imp of sin;
No crimes had ever known.
They took the shaggy stranger in
And reared him as their own.

.   .   .   .

Many a laugh went through the vale;
And some conviction too—
Each thought some other Goblin tale,
Perhaps was just as true.

ROBERT BLOOMFIELD, 1806
From a traditional Fakenham story

CHAPTER 14

Stolen sweets are always sweeter,
Stolen kisses much completer,
Stolen looks are nice in chapels;
Stolen, stolen be your apples.

THOMAS RANDOLPH

WELL, my Keepering Job had come to a finish as I have told, and as had hapened to me sevrell times before I had to start fresh and make a liven. I supose I did not worry much about that as I always knew I could get on without a regular Job. I had had a fairly easy life and I did not seam to trubble, and so of corse in the end I had to have a go at the Game again.

In them days there was one man that I used to go out with. I have not met many men in my time that I took up with, but there have been lots that wanted to pall up with me. Some said they knew all the Points about Poaching, and others said they wanted to learn. Or they would come and tell me they were hard up and the Children starving, and I have given many of them a cupple of shillings to be quit of them. I knew too much to want that sort along with me. Besides I did not care to find all the cake so that they might eat half. A lot of them were Just Pot hunters, and Lazey men. The farm Labourer is diffrent, he will catch a hare wen he can as that mean a good dinner for his family, and no one can blame him for that, wen meat dinners are hard to come by.

So I took up with a pall and as there was not much about the Game I did not know by that time, I played the King of the Norfolk Poachers for all I was worth. After a little while the place got too warm for me, and I decided to move, and I kept on moving from place to place. As sone as one got to hot I moved to another, and so I shifted about Norfolk, but always carried the Game on to some extent.

There are many as may say haven left the Game I had no need to go back to it, and that may be so, but as I have said before I think it was born in me.

I do not think that lots of People can help what they do. We see well to do folks go in a shop, and steal some verry useless artickle which they could buy for a small amount if they liked, but they do it. It is put down to a sudden lapse and it may be so, but I think it is fate and they canot help it. I have known men to steal the most useless things but it seam they could not help it some how.

Then you se some People try to get on in the World, and try there utmost, and still they cannot do anything they want. Another man never seam to try, but everything go rite with him, and he can't do rong, Fortune favours everything he do.

Any way I went back to the Game. Perhaps it was hard on my wife, but she got used to it, and I had got a second child to keep by then. The girl was born when we had been about eighteen months married, but she was twelve years old wen the boy came.

The children did a lot to settle my wife, but she never did like Norfolk being Lancashire born. Evrything was strange to her, and so much Diffrent to Lancashire ways. She could not onderstand our ways and talk, neither could my old People onderstand hers, try as they would. It used to make her verry fretfull at first, she missed the sound of traffick and the noise of Manchester, and all that was doing. But wen our first Baby came she grew more content, but she would try and lern it the Lancashire way of speech as soon as it could talk.

She was verry fond of animiles and birds, ferritts and dogs, like my first wife had been, so we got on well together, but somehow it was not like my first marrage—there always seamed some thing short with me. My memries used to hike back to the old days, although I never showed it to her, but I knew then there is no love like the first.

After a time I went to a place close to Wells were there were hundreds of hars. I sone lerned the way about there and got a great many of them with no one any the wiser. I only stayed there one year to live, but I knew the way back and did well there for a long time. No one knew I traveled that way after I left, as wen you go Poaching it is as well to rember to cover your tracks.

That is one way the old Green roads come in useful, the ones the smugglers used. There are a great many Green roads in Norfolk, but it is not so often they get used these days, the time for them has gone.

There is one running from Wormagay Bridge straight to Swaffham, it catch Pentney, West Billney, and Marham on the way, and then on to Swaffham heath and Narbrough. Of corse it is hardly discernuble in some places, but it is a Publick foot path all the way.

In diffrent Parishes it has diffrent names. At West Bilney it is called the Warren Path, in Pentney it is called Dales Drove, in Marham the Fen lane, outside Marham but still in Marham bounds the Ramper, till it get to Swaffham heath, it is then called Swaffham Road. Then it go on to Pickenham just touching Beachamwell and then still go on.

No doubt it was one of the Ancient roads as some times it is thirty feet wide, at other places it is mearly a foot path.

There is another Green road running over Grimstone Comon. I do not know were it begin, but I know that it go on to Lynn on one side through Barsey and after leaving Grimstone it run on to Gayton Thorpe and East Walton, and away to Southacre and Westacre and then on the Castle Acre. Like the others it is called by diffrent names but the old People always spoke of it as Pot Row.

Many is the time I have traveled them Green roads. Of corse they have tried to abolish them old roads by Plowing them up wen they run over Private land. Just as this road enter Walton Field there is a verry large mound thirty feet high. The old People used to say a great Battle was fought there, any how the plough was always turning up bones and rusty bits of mettall in my time.

Then there is the Pedders way through Norfolk. I do not know were it begin nor yet were it end, all I know is I have traced it from Fincham by Downham Market to Marham, Shuldam and across Narbrough field. It is called Devells Dyke on Narbrough field and is some four feet in hight there. Then it travel on to the bounds of Narford, but of corse in many places it is almost gone, were the plough have been over it.

It cross Narford Estate a verry wide green lane. The late Algeron Fountain once planted it over with small trees and railed it up and thought I supose to be rid of it, but as other foot paths run into it there was a lot of trubble and he had to pull them all up. That was some forty years ago.

Pedders way then run on to Narford, just catch a bit of Westacre, and then on to Castle Acre and Newton, Merton, and I belive to Thetford passing through many villiges on the way. My old Grandfather have told me that the Smugglers used all these Green roads and by ways to smugle there Contraband goods, and that they had there holes and hiden places all along these routs. Were I was Keeper we had a verry large Warren beside the road running from Wormagay. One day the warriners were digging at the botom of a large hill were Oliver Cromwell was suposed to have planted his guns wen he destroyed Pentney Abby, and they came on a large hole about four yards square, which it was plain to be seen had been all timbered up many years before. A Gentleman came and looked at it and said it was one of the Smuglers hides.

In all my sixty years at night work I do not think I ever was frigtened but once, and that was one night wen I was out after those Hars. I had done fairly well and had to cross a large field with a farm Premises in the middle such as you often find in Norfolk. They always used to say this place was Haunted, but as I never belived in that sort of thing I was not trubbling. The moon was Just up and casten long shadows, and as I came round the corner of the buildings into the shadow, I sudenly saw the most terreble looking monster you could emadgine. The eyes shone full into my eyes, and dear Reader I was so frigtened I seam to sweat cold

sweat. I dare not go away, nor go any nearer to it, and there I stood
rooted to the ground. At last it moved and turned away from me into
the moonlight, and I saw it was a red and white bullock. It was its ears
that kept moven that made it look so horiblle.

It was a foolish thing but it was a long time before I got over that
fright. Of corse I have been startled at times by comen onto things but
never like that, it give me a reglar turnup.

Every old house had its haunt in them days, not that many people
dont belive it to day, but I for one never did belive in any thing super-
natrall nor Witch craft after I begun to
think for myself. As I have said I have been
out as much as any one at nights, but I have
never seen any thing I did not make out
what it was in the end. True some times
diffrent objects take a fantastic shape at
night in diffrent lights.

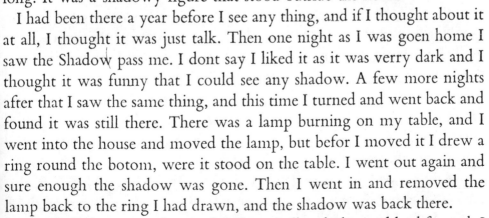

When I was Keepering I lived in a lodge
that evry one said was haunted. The Old
man that lived there before me told me so
and that he did not doubt but what I should se it befor I had been there
long. It was a shadowy figure that stood outside the house.

I had been there a year before I see any thing, and if I thought about it
at all, I thought it was just talk. Then one night as I was goen home I
saw the Shadow pass me. I dont say I liked it as it was verry dark and I
thought it was funny that I could see any shadow. A few more nights
after that I saw the same thing, and this time I turned and went back and
found it was still there. There was a lamp burning on my table, and I
went into the house and moved the lamp, but befor I moved it I drew a
ring round the botom, were it stood on the table. I went out again and
sure enough the shadow was gone. Then I went in and removed the
lamp back to the ring I had drawn, and the shadow was back there.

The window was made up of diffrent Collered glass and lead framed. I found the pane I wanted and removed it, and the shadow was never seen again. It had been seen for a great many years, but that was the explanation of that gost and it seam as if I had laid it by a little investergation.

I have not the least doubt that if people investergated the diffrent things that they have seen and heard they would have found what puzled them as simple.

I was never frightened if I got into a tight corner and the Keepers were round me. That is the time the Poacher want to keep coole, and have all his witts about him.

I have laid and seen the Keepers go past me many a time. On one ocation I was in a wood at Whaton and three keepers were looking for me. I had killed a bird within a few yards of them. While they were looking for me I got out of the Wood and shot all the way home.

Of corse it is a useless Job looking for one man in a wood wen it is dark, he have only to lay down or stand still and let those that are looken pass him.

In a generell way the Keepers are a lot more excited than the Poacher. I have often smiled to myself wen I have got away to think what a stew they were in, wen they found me gone. If I have had a gun I have often fired it to let them know that I was gone and wich way.

It is a rum Job for the Keepers to catch a lone Poacher wen it is dark. One time I rember I was surounded by Keepers, I could hear them talking while I was layen there quite still, and as sone as I could I drew away from them and they never heard me or knew I was there.

I was verry fairly sucessful in getten away from keepers, and if this should meet the eye of some of them they will rember the times I have hoodwinked them. I do not think they bare me any anomosity for all that, in fact they are always frendly with me.

It is often not Keepers as gets you into trubble. One night about this time I was comen home over some grass fields, it was verry dark with no moon. Suddenly I stumbled on a horse lyen on the ground. He Jumped up and my nose came in contact with his hip bone,—result a broken nose for me.

Another night me and my pall had been out, and were comen home by a foot path wich was a right of way. The farmer had tried to stop people using it, and had turned out a verry vicious Bull with his cows on the medow. As we went past the Bull got up and began blowing. My mate went on ahead, and the bull started to follow him, so as sone as he got a fair distance from me I gave him a cupple of charges in the hind quarters.

They found him in a pit in the corner of the field next morning dead, but as no one saw it done and no one herd the shots, that sone blew over.

Another Job we did ended in a bit of a joke. Near by there was a big Hall with a sort of Ornermental fish Pond beside it, with some verry fine trout in it. The water was quite shallow, not more than a foot deep.

Well those fish were talked

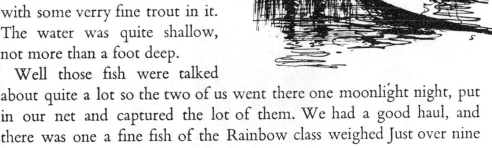

about quite a lot so the two of us went there one moonlight night, put in our net and captured the lot of them. We had a good haul, and there was one a fine fish of the Rainbow class weighed Just over nine Pound.

We got the fish to Lynn befor they were missed, but a few days after I saw in the paper that a Gentleman had caught a fine trout wich he was haven stuffed,—I knew the fisherman verry well.

I went and asked the dealer who he had sold the big fish we had cought to, and it was the same Gentleman that had caught the fish—so much for his Catchen it.

It was wonderful how things changed hands about those parts, if there was any Prise fowls about they were sone plentifull in other places. There was a Gentleman close to ower villige with some kind of black forren ducks,[1] not quite black, more of a bronse coller. He was verry perticular over them but by the next year they were plentiful at other places, some of his eggs haven been stolen.

There are a lot of the Present day Poachers will steal fowles or anything that come to hand, but I can safely say I never stole a fowl with all the things I have done, except the Pea fowl which I have told about.

[1] These were probably the Black East Indian Ducks belonging to the late Sir William ffolkes, Bart., of Hillingdon. He *was* 'very particular' about them. As a child I owned a pair he gave me, but unlike most ducks they were very polygamous in their habits, mating with even wild duck that came down and not disdaining the farm-yard inhabitants, so it was almost impossible to keep the strain pure.—L. R. H.

CHAPTER 15

THE FEMALE CABIN BOY

It is of a pretty Female as you shall understand,
She had a mind for roving, into some foreign land;
Attired in sailor's clothing, she boldly did appear,
And engaged her with a Captain, to serve him for one year.

She engaged her with a Captain his cabin boy to be,
The wind it being in favour, they soon put out to sea;
The Captain's lady was on board, her face was lit with joy,
That her husband had engaged for her, so handsome a cabin boy.

His cheeks were like the red rose, his side locks they did curl,
The sailors used to laugh and say, 'He look just like a girl.'
But eating sailor's biscuits her colour did destroy,
And the waist did swell of pretty Nell, our female cabin boy.

One night among the sailors there was a jolly row,
As through the Bay of Biscay, their gallant ship did plough;
They bundled from their hammocks, it did their rest destroy,
To hear the dreadful groaning of the female cabin boy.

The Doctor ran with all his might, smiling at the fun,
To think a sailor lad should have a daughter or a son.
'The child belongs to none of us', the sailors they did swear,
And stuck to the declaration when a daughter she did bear.

Then said the Captain to his wife, 'My dear I wish you joy,
'Tis either you or I betrayed our handsome cabin boy'.
Then each took up a bumper, and drank success to trade,
And to their handsome cabin boy, who was neither man nor maid.

Obtained in MS. from the Author

CHAPTER 15

As he walked along to work
And saw his landlord's game
Devour his master's crops,
He thought it was a shame.
But if the Keeper found on him
A rabbit or a wire;
He got it hot, when brought before
The Parson and the Squire.

Old Poaching Song

THERE was many a man asked me in those days what he had to lern to be a Professnial Poacher, and they mostly got the same answer. By experence he have to lern and he may lern a lot, but he want a lot of experience befor he can become a fairly sucessful man. In them days I was not giving away anything, but now they are passed for me it dont matter, and I will try and tell most of what I lernt.

The first thing is to keep a still tunge in your head, as some young beginers get excited and begin to brag. Well nothing anoy a keeper more than to hear of some one bragin in a Public house of what he have done, and the keeper is shure to try and catch him, as he is thinking his Master may hear of it and want to know why he is not looking after his business. Besides it let evryone know his trade and put People wise to him.

Its a true word that the days of the Professnial Poacher is gone. True there are a few pot hunters still about, but the young man of to day think more of his foot Ball and other kinds of sport, and I am not shure that they are not a lot better off.

Befor I have finished I think dear Reader you will agree that the Poacher is as clever as most other men. True he is an outlaw against the Laws of the land, but that do not disturb him much, but rather give him more encuragment than not.

If the Poacher work alone it is a hard Job for the Keeper to run him to earth, that is if the poacher use a little comon sence.

He will have a lot to lern as I have said befor. He must study wether, and all the signs of wood craft, the call of birds, and the flight of Wood Pigons in the wood at night, and distinguish the diffrent sounds, and there are a lot of diffrent sounds in the woods at night, and other rough places.

Wen he enters a wood he must get the wind in his face, and take pertucler notice wich point it blows from, or he is some lost and must travel his ground over again, to no Purpose. The wind and the stars are his guide. If I was to sit down in the middle of a large wood and I could see the stars, I could easly find my way. Foggy wether is the worst the Poacher have to face, it may be clear wen he enter the wood, but the fogg lead him astray, and he may have a hard Job to find his way out. If he once loses himself he is lost, as evrything look alike to him.

A Poacher is worth all he get. A great many People would be surprised if they only knew what the poacher is asked to get for some People, aspeshilly wen the game is out of season. A good many Farmers shut there eyes to the Poacher, they know he will shut gates after him, besides them gettin a brace of Birds now and again. So long as the Poacher let his fowles alone he do not bother much about him. Also a good Poacher never disturb a flock of sheep if he can help it, as he know there is nothing for him were the sheep are folded. Some Shepperds are fool enough to try and give the Poacher away—silly on there part, as the Poacher can do him a lot of harm, and he is none the wiser till the harm is done.

Well now I will try and tell how the Poacher work. There are many ways of taking Phesants and other game, the gun, the hingle or snare, the trap, and the net. Wen the Poacher enter a wood as I have said befor he goes with the wind in his face, as Phesants always sit facen the wind, to keep there feathers down. He draws along as quietly as Possible till he se his bird, then crall with in shot of it and kill it.

Years ago we used to use a sight of this kind. Cut a pair of ears out of a stuff pice of leather and use it on the muzzle of the gun—so it look like rabbits ears on the end.

Wen the Poacher could se the bird between the ears he was shure of his kill, but since then the Eleuminated sight is much more used, and the four point ten gun. I have tried it with a lot of sucess. The gun in the old days was the muzle loder

with the Barrells cut off to eighteen inches, and as small a bore as we could get, mostly sixteen bore.

First I will tell the different ways of taking Phesants. As I have said, first the gun at night, next the hingle or snare. The snare is used were the Phesants creep through hedges, a bow stick being put round the Hingle to make the bird drop his head. Another way is to make a hole in the ground three inch deep and two inch across the top. The hingle is laid round the hole that have already been partly filled with white peas. He come along and put his head in the hole, bring the hingle up on his neck and is verry sone dead.

A nother way is to take a strong steel trap and run hot pitch on the plate, and put some peas on the pitch. The bird come and pick at the peas, and is caught by the head and killed instantly. The hingle is also used in the hare and rabbitt runs in the long grass in a wood with a bender over the hingle, to keep his head down to the level of the snare.

The hingle for Phesants is made of four strands of plible copper wire, as sone as he pull the wire tight he is dead.

If the hare come she jump the bar, the Phesant go through and is caught. There are hundreds of Phesants caught by the net, that is how the Dealer have them by the first of October—they are caught by the

Partridge netter. In the old days the Poacher would clear a path in an outlayen wood, and then run a net across. By that way he would take a lot of Birds, but them Jobs are over now, as the old fashioned Poaching days are over. There was more game destroyed in one season then than there are in ten now by the so called pot hunter. The Poacher of to day have not the nerve they had fifty years ago.

Now I will try and tell how the Partridges are taken. The netter goes round and listen for the Partridges calling each other up at roosting time.

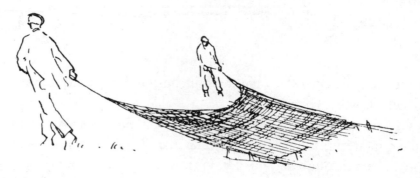

He knows were the birds are layen by that way, and make his plans acorden to the weather. If it is light he wait till the night is dark and dry befor he go out.

The birds mostly sleep on barley stubble or thin grass. He know prety well were the birds are layen and go along quiet and draw his net against the wind and he is prety shure of the lot of them. If they should raise befor the net cover them, he pick them up two or three at a time as they are scattered about in the dark.

The net is about twenty five yards long, and ten feet deep, with a mesh of two inches and it take two good strong men to draw it over the land if it is whet, as there is a lot of weight to pull.

The upper part of the net is kept clear of the ground. I have often seen fifteen or Eighteen in the net at once. The netter can tell as sone as he have covered his birds by the flutter and shruck [shriek].

The Phesant is a most vicious bird, I have seen the young cocks fight

nd kill the old ones many a time. They will eat any thing, mice, frogs
nd any kind of carrion, nothing comes amiss to him, but like dirty
ducks they are good eating. The hen is a most curageous bird in the
defence of her young, and I have seen her drive both stoats and rats
way from them fighting with both wings and feet, and besides she will
pick at her enimies.

Well, to go on with the way to take Partriges. Wen the season is
advanced, say December, the Poachers look round first at dark, and find
were there is a covey of Birds sleeping. Then he take some small wheat
nd boiled oats, and scatter the corn about twenty five yards from a
headge or ditch, dropping a few drops of Oile of Carryway seed on the
corn. As sone as the Poacher find that the birds have found the feed he
get there before it is light with his gun. He know as sone as the birds are
on foot, and wen they all get on the feed he empties boath of his Barrells
n amongst them, and some times he get eight or ten of them at the one
go. Of corse he gether them up as quickly as posible and get out. If the
keeper hear the shots and make for the spot, the man is a long way away
befor he get there.

Another way is wen the ground is covered with snow and there is a
good moon the Poacher dresses up in a white sute. He will find his birds
n snowy wether on the lea of a hill or lyen in a low place. He creep up
o them with the wind in his face, and wen he is within shot give a low
wistle. The birds raise there heads—and that is his chance. I had a kind of
lop made with a hood, so that there were only my eyes clear. I have
killed twenty birds at a time some nights, and a hare or two wen the
wether have been sharp, and I have stood still. Of corse this Job is all
verry well, but it show up on the snow and you must not try it too often,
not in the same place any ways.

You can some times get a whole covey of birds on a foggy morning if
you are under a hedge, and can keep out of sight of them, as the Birds
hat are not hurt keep running round the wounded ones, and you may
get the lot if you dare stay long enough.

Some four years ago, a Chap in London rote to the Daily Male, and said it was a splendid time for the Partrige netter, as the moon was as bright as day on the first of September, and the Poacher could se to lay his net over the Birds. Well, I rote to that Chap and told him if he would come to my place I would show him that what he knew of the Job was not much. Well, he rote back and said that that was what he had been told. I think that a great many people rite what they are told on lots of subjects. The man that has experinced these things are the ones that know how it is done.

Now I will try and tell how the Hars and Rabbitts are taken by the Poacher; the snare and the trap, the gate net and the long net. The snare for hars is mostly set in the runs that they make across land or in the Hedge rowes. The run throw the hedge is called the muse. It is much more difficult to snare the hare in the hedge than on the paths she make, as the hare stop at a hedge and look round to se if any enimies are lurkin there, but she Job along her run any old how, taken no notice of any

thing. The best way at the Hedge is to lay a piece of white paper in one muse and lay a snare in the next one. She se the paper and run to the next muse, bolt throw, and is easly killed.

The snare in the run is held up with a small stick called the pricker, it is put eight inches high from the ground, which is the height he carry his head. The snare is made up of six or eight strands of cooper wire, with a strong cord ring attached to the stake. For the rabbitt the wire is fower inches high. The rabbitt run is much diffrent to the hars run—it is made in pads, as the rabbitt hop along, wile the hare galloppe,—a lot of diffrence. The snare is put were his feet is put, he stand his proper height and is caught round the neck. If the snare is propply fixed he sone choke himself to death.

There was a Lady given some Lectures at Norwich some three years ago, about the crulty of trapping rabbitts. No doubt there is a lot of crulty. I was snaring and trapping rabbitts at the time, and as she stated a lot of things she did not onderstand, I set down and rote to that Lady, and tryed to explean some of the things to her. I think she said that the Keepers on Lady Suffeld estate were not alowed to use the steel trap. She said that they got the best shotts and shott the rabbitts. I asked what become of the wounded ones? Was it not better to catch the rabbitt and kill it out of hand than let it lay and suffer.

Well, she sent me a dozen of her humane snars—the rabbitt would live for days if one did not go to them. In mine they are dead in a few minuts—but the Lady like a lot more People, knew what some one told her and I have always found that facts were better things.

Well, now I will tell you how to train the Dogs, as for netten rabbitts and hars one must have a dog. The best breed of dogs are a cross between the Smithfield cattle dog and the Greyhound, as you get the greyhound speed and the Smithfield sence, and there are no breed of dogs with the sagasity of the Smithfield. The pup must have a broad head across the eyes, as that is were he keep his brains, deep chest, sturdy legs and plenty of coat. The longer he can keep on his mother the stronger he get, the bitch will know wen to wean him.

At the age of four months he may begin his lerning. First get a rabbitt skin and stuff it with some thing soft, wading is the best. Take the pup out and throw the skin for him to bring to you. He will sone lern that. Wen he bring it to you reward him with a piece of sugar, but on no account alow him to play with it. If he is that way inclined punish him, but not severly.

As sone as you find that he will bring the skin to you hide it up in the Hedge and let him find it, that will lern him to seek for his game later on. Do not let him run game, anyhow till he is eight months old, or he may

find that he canot catch a rabbitt, and that make him think it is no us
running after it.

Then get a live rabbitt and take it to a large field, were the rabbit
have a long way to get to hide, then let the puppy have his chance. We

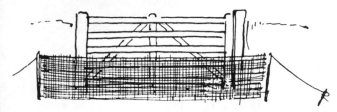

he find that he can catch h
game he will never refuse t
run after it again.

Well that is his first lessor
the next is to lern him to fin
his owen game, and to ler
him the net. For that you want another dog trained to the Job. Th
trained dog will soon lern the pup, and the young dog will take
delight in trying to keep up with the old un. Wen you find tha
the young one begins to hunt well, you take him out wen there i
a bit of moonlight for a trial. If you can find a place were the rabbitt
have been wired in by wire netting, that is the place to give him hi
first lesson with the rabbitt net.

Put the rabbitt net as close to the wire as you can get, as no matte
how you try to keep the rabbitts in, there are always some get over th
Wire netting. Well the object of running the rabbitt net against the wire
netting is to lern the dog to stop. As soon as he come to the net he i
rash at first, but wen he find that the wire hurt his nose, he will lern t
jump the net and nip his rabbitt on the other side, and will never nock
the net over.

The rabbitt net is about sixty yards long and thirty inches wide o
deep, and is held by eight stakes eighteen inches high. The Poacher carries
the stakes in a sheeth, and he have a pretty tough job with a young dog,
as he have to hold his dog and stake up his net at the same time. But the
dog soon get to know that he must not go till he is told to go.

Wen the net is ready the poacher stand at one end of the net with his
hand on the top. By that means he know directly a rabbitt is in the net,
as he can feel it kicking, and go and kill it.

Of corse wen his dog can find no more game he pick up his net and go further along. I have killed six and eight Dozen Rabbitts on a good night, with a bit of luck.

Now to lern the young dog the gate net. If you have an old dog he will lern the young same as he will the other game. You take the pair of them and put the net behind the gate, and the two dogs hunt the field until they find a hare. The old dog will drive her to the gate and she is caught there in the net, but the young dog will have a bite at her to. He will sone know were to drive the hare as he finds out that the gate is were he can catch her. The net is seven yards long and three feet deep, put up with two wing pieces to it.

You must not let the young dog work too long, but give him a rest and a bit of something to eat. The old dog well know wen to rest him self.

I had one old dog so perfectly trained, if he walked to a field gate he knew well enough if there was a hare on that field. He would just whine and stand still till the net was ready, and the hare would be quickly dead. Me and that dog killed hundreds of hars and rabbitts. I kept him till like me he could not work any longer. If there was a Keeper or a Police-man about he knew, and would let me know as plain as if he could speak.

I have been ofered a lot of monies for him, but he was never for sale. He trained a lot of young dogs for me in his day, for which I have made some good prices. I have had a great many dogs but none like him—he had no faults and its a Job to find a dog with out one fault, like a lot else in this world.

I had another, a small retrever bitch, I trained for the gun at night. She could find a Phesant up a tree as well as I could, all I had to do was to watch her, and she would find them. As sone as the bird was killed I had it in my hand, but like a lot of useful things she died before she was verry old. I well rember goen in a wood not far from Bungay. I shot a bird from a tree and the bitch brought it to me growling. There were two Keepers within twenty yards of me, but I simply crawled in the wood and laid down and they passed me by.

My memry often goes back to them days, wen I played the game all out and made a good thing out of it for many years. Well, I think to myself, I have had my share of pleasure and my share of trubbles, and now I am alone and my work nearly done, and I must make myself content until the finish. I have rote these lines and told what I know, not to lern the young man of to day the art of taken game but Just to show how one man can dupe a lot of others. I am now seventy five, and if I had my time to come over again I would still be what I have been—A Poacher.

CHAPTER 16

THE MISER'S DAUGHTER

There was an old Miser in London did dwell,
He had but one daughter who a Sailor loved well,
When the old Miser was out of the way
She would court the young Sailor by night and by day.

But when the old Miser heard what she had dared
Straight way to a Captain he immediately fared
Saying 'Captain, bold Captain, good news I've to tell,
I've got a young Sailor as transport to sell'.

When the fair lady she heard of the news,
To the Captain she hastened to tell him her views,
Saying 'Captain, bold Captain, I've bad news to tell,
You have got my young Sailor as transport to sell'.

Out of her pockets she threw handfuls of gold
Which on his main deck immediately rolled,
Saying 'Captain, bold Captain, all this I give you
For my jolly young sailor, he's my right and my due'.

'Oh no, fairest lady, that never can be,
He was sold yesterday as a transport to me.
I've a wife and three daughters who will hark to his moan,
Give him fair greeting, and welcome him home.'

'If you have shipped him and sailed him right over the main,
So he will never come back to court me again,
I'll hie my way home to lie alone on my bed,
For now to my Sailor I'll never be wed.

'My heart it is broken, it will never be spring,
Though the blackbird do whistle and the nightingale sing;
Bad luck to my parents wherever they be,
For I know in my heart they have ruined me.'

MS. from the Author

160

CHAPTER 16

Beccles for a Puritan,
Bungay for the Poor,
Halesworth for a Drunkard
And Bliborough for a Whore.

Old Local Proverb

Time went on and I found as I had to move again and this time a bit further a field. How I came to Suffolk do not matter, but come I did, and I have no fault to find with it and have lived here up to the present time, much the same way as I did before, until I begun to feel my years. Dont think that I finished with the game—the game finished with me. I wold give ten years of my life time to see the last forty years come Back—but I cant so Fiddle dun De.

Many people think that a Poacher is a bit of a slack, perhaps some are. They put him down as a lazey drunken fellow, but Dear Reader, beleve me, a Professnial Poacher is anything but that. He is a hard worken man. It is no easy Job to pull a thirty yard bird net over stubbles, and I have been whet through with sweat many times. It is just as hard work netten rabbitts, its the getten them away there. I have had to carry as many as four dozen at a time, acros Cuntry, over hedges and ditches, as it is the Poacher's rule never to get on a road if he can help it, and four dozen rabbitts weigh a bit.

Well, I have had some good times round Bungay, and killed some hundreds of Phesants one time and another and had some good jokes to. There was a Gentleman well known round about, and he thought he would like to have a bit of sport, and excitement. I said verry well sir, if you will go with me you shall have all the excitment you wish for. I called for him and off we went, I am not goen to say were, but within two miles of Bungay. I sone found a bird and killed it, and he said had we not best be goen. I told him it would be time enough to think of goen wen we had had a good few more shots, and kept him on the go and let him carry all the game.

About fower in the morning I said now I think we had better be making ower way home. He wanted to know were we were, I said Close to were

the Nuns are, but there is just one more place I must call but not at the Nunery. We got through a large hedge, and he said again were the Hell are we? I told him we were in a Gentleman's Orchid. I think that I killed a brace of birds there and then made for home. I took him over land and marshes but got him home safe. Well, he said, if that is Poaching I would not have another night at it for fifty pounds.

There is a Rectory not far from were we went that night and on a nother ocasion I was out and shot a Phesant just by the Clergman's window. I had picked the bird up, when up went the window and the Revrend John's head come out, and he said 'What are you after in my garden?' I knew he could not se me, so I told him it was all rite, I was not touchen nothen belongen to him, and should not hurt him, and he said all right, Good morning and shut the window. He was a grand old Gentleman still alive, but have left that viccerage now and live in Bungay.

On another night I was up at St. John's and had left my bicicle on the road by the Church wall. Wen I come back what should I se but the Vicker a weelen my bike away. Of corse I verry sone wanted to know what the —— he ment stealing of my bike like that. I put the wind up him considable, took the bike befor he could think any more about it,

Jumped on and rid away. If he knew me he never made any row about it and I had many birds from there befor and after that.

There was a nother Joke I had over that bicicle when P.C. Stammers was stationed at Bungay and that is not so verry long ago. I lived in Bridge Street at that time and had got my bike ready to go out one evening. He saw it standing in the yard and thought that was fine, he would watch it and se me go out and catch me good and proper. I put a bag on the bike and a lamp, and then went to a frend and borrowd another and went out as I had ment, leaven Stammers to watch mine as long as he plesed. He knew I was out of the house some were, and wen I came home in the erly morning I found the bike gone. I smiled to my self as I thought I knew well enough were it was. I went to Stammers next morning to report the loss, but befor I got through with that I started to laugh. I will not say here what he said to me, but he had stayed there fower mortal howers watchen the bike and waiten for me to go out. Of corse he would have folowed me were I went as he knew it was no use him tryen to have me wen I came home, as I never brought any thing home with me in the morning, I knew better as he had tried that to often.

It was while I was liven in Bridge Street that I was goen home in the evning time, and met the Sargent on the Falcon Bridge. He stopped me and took a Phesant from me and my gun, and sumonsed me for haven game in my Posession, onlawfully obtained. He did not ask me were I got it from or any thing like that. Wen I got up to the Cort the Cheerman asked me were I got it from, I told him that I found it on Bungay Comon, and that they had been shooting on Arsham [Earsham] Estate that day, just over the river. The Sargent ask me why I did not tell him that befor, so I said 'Ah! Sargent you did not ask me'. As I had a witness I got clear of that, and then I asked for my gun and bird back, which I got, but they had skined the bird so that was no use to me. The Cheerman said, 'Well, we will dismiss the case, but we have our own Idea about it'—so had I. I often asked the Sargent how he had enjoyed it after that.

I should like to set down here that I Claim to be the only one that made the late Sir Rider Haggard laugh on the Chair. A Police man had had me up for haven a Phesant and a Partridge in my Posesion. Well I had to apear before the Bench and they could not tell were I had got them from. At last Sir Rider ask what about the People that I got them from I told him that I had killed hundreds of Phesants but never killed on with its name on its tail, and of corse that made him laugh.

I owed them some thing like a pound so Mr. Sprake [the Clerk] asked me wen I was goen to pay. I told him I was like the Scotch Salmon Poacher he said he would pay wen the salmon came up the river, so told Mr. Sprake I would pay wen the Phesants came into season agin.

As the Police said I had harped on the rite String that time. But Sir Rider told me I must pay a pound, wich I thought was verry Jenerous of him.

I think I have paid something like twenty pound in fines since I have been in Suffolk. The last time I was up for the Job at Lodon they charged me 20 Schillings, but comen home I shot five Phesants. Little I cared for them or there fines as long as they give me my gun and Chartriges—and I thought I might as well use them wen the chance offered.

So things went along some times well some times not so well, but Poacher can most times make a liven. There is not much come amiss to him so long as he can keep the Police bussy, and as long as he keep still tunge in his head he is all rite. The man that go laughen about wha he have done is sone found out, and he find that them that laugh la have the best of the laugh. A great many People wold be surprised to know what the Poacher is asked to do for other People, as they thin that he is an outlaw and they make a Tool of him as much as they chose Well he sone find out who he may serve, and Who to tell to do ther own Dirty work there selves.

I well rember haven been asked by a Gentleman to get him a brac of hars, of corse I sone got them, but I was a bit down on him, and too them to him alive. Wen I got there I told him I had got the hars and go

he price off him. Wen I gave him the Hars, he said, 'kill them for me'.
told him to kill them for himself. For years after he was called All
Alive. If I had killed them he would have had me for killing game with
out a licence, as I had been a bit of a trubble to him in the past. There
was no law for taken Hars alive, but the killing was another matter.

Wen times was bad I have turned my atention to Musherooms, and
wen the arly frosts set into Wallnutts, they all have there markett if you
know were to look for it and them. Then in some parts of Norfolk
here are the trout in the season, as there used to be a ready and good sale
or those fish. The way was to put a net down and drag another net
towards it, in that way a Poacher would sone clear a stream of trout
and other corse fish. If there was a pond that contained carp and tench,
the plan was to get some stone bottles, fill them partly full of lime broken
small, and cork them up, cutting a small slit in the cork, wiren the cork
down at the same time. This alowed a little water to drain in, and then
they were thrown in the pond. Wen the water got into the bottles they
burst, and the concushon and the lime brought the fish to the top of the
water, were they were easly landed with a net.

Many is the time too wen I could not get about so well I did a bit of
mole catchen for the Farmers round, moles bein a rare lot of trubble in
some pastures, and if left alone will breed at a great rate, so must be
kept down.

In the old days there was a lot of supistition regarden this small Animile
and still is in a lot of places. Many years ago the people gave it a lot of
riverince. They would carry the mole's fore feet in there pockets as a
prevention for Cramp[1] and other Ailments,—the fore legs if the arms
are bad, but if you were bad in the legs it must be the hind ones. They
used to say if you wore the wrong ones you would soon have the complaint in the same limbs. Also that to eat a mole was a shure Cure for a
weak bladder, but if a person be a feamale she must eat the male mole,

[1] A local cure is to put the sufferer's boots 'one coming and one going' at the foot of the bed.—
L. R. H.

and if a male the feamale. I have been asked many times for one or the other for that purpose.

There is lots of people say that moles only move and work at chiming howers [*i.e.* four, eight, twelve], but I have never found it that way, the mole like other Animiles work wen he is hungrey. I have caught them at all howers of the day, and have killed many hundreds in my time. It is true they hunt for worms more in the early howers of the morning, the reason being that the night dews bring the worms nearer the surface of the ground. This may be seen if any one walk on the medaws in the evening or early morning, as they will see the worms on the top of the land and grass medaws—they are called dew worms.

I used to be very sucessful catchen moles, but I seldom used traps. In the fore part of the spring, on beet and corn land, I found that I could kill a lot more by walking slowely and quittley about the land. Wen they are working for food you may ditect them severell yards away from you by the fresh mould they are throwing up.

They will work a lot after a shower of rain wen the sun come out again. It is not generley known that the mole lay up a store of worms for sharp wether, but he do. They will get hundreds of worms and store them in there old nests—they Just bite the worms head and leave them for further use.

Moles are good fore tellers of heavy rains as then they leave the low land and go up to the higher land befor the floods come.

If you use traps the best runs to trap them in is by the sides of drains and hedges, as they seem to go to the Hedge and the drains verry often in the twenty four hours. You may trap them were they cross a gate way or path, but wen a mole gets in a garden he take a lot of catchen by the Amature any way. The best way is to find the run at the Garden gate or in the path, but of cors it take a lot of experince to find what is termed the main run. Dear Reader you must forgive me if I run on a bit on my Subject, but it take years to know the way of Animiles.

The blood of the mole is a shure cure for warts on the hands or any part of the boddy. Get a mole alive, and Just tap him on the head, and he will bleed at the nose. Rub the blood on the warts, burry the mole and the warts will disappear. I have tried it many times and have never known it to fail. It is hundreds of years old that cure, but many people have forgot it.

The best time of the year to catch moles in traps is from February to March, wen they are on the run. They rush up and down the runs looking for the female, and wen the males meet there are some terreble battles. They will come on the top of the land and fight till the death. I have put two of them in a tub and watched them fight, one of them will sone die.

I once had a tame one in a wood box with a glass top. It was verry amusin to see him playen in the mould. He would eat twenty or thirty worms a day. I used to try him with all sorts of insects, but never saw him eat any thing except the worm. It have been said that the mole do a lot of good and destroy many wire worms, and the lavare of the Billywitch or Cockchafer but I do not think so, as I have never found anything only the remains of earth worms in there insides; but I do not think there is any one will be able to tell the exact truth about the mole.

After we have had a lot of frost and snow, wen you se the mole put up he arth it is a shure sign that the frost is breaking up. Hot and long dry weather kill thousands of moles as they cannot stand the dry for they cannot get there food and cannot work as fast as the worm, which goes deep down in the earth. I have seen many times the mole worken under the surface and the worm comen out on top a yard before the mole. I think they more depend on the worms falling in the runs, than what they can work to.

I do not think there is any thing will prey on the mole except the fox, but nature have so ordered it that evry thing have some enimies, if not lots of those Pests would ruin the Cuntry side, but nature have seen to all that. Dogs will catch them but not eat them even if they are skined.

I belive that the mole is the strongest of any Animile acorden to size, I have frequently stood on him in the ground, and he will heave your legs

up. People say the mole rout and break the ground with his fore feet, an
lift it up with his nose and head.

After the Great War there skins were of good value, I have made tw
and six for a single skin. Now they send them from France, Holland an
Belgium and other Cuntries so they are of little value and scarse worth th
Catchin, and skining. Wen they were streched square they had to mesur
seven inches long and five across to get the best price.

There are three diffrent spices of moles. I have caught cream coloure
ones and some with a sandy stripe down the midle of the Body. On som
lands the moles are verry large, and on others verry small, but I never sav
a white one yet.

CHAPTER 17

GILES COLLINS AND LADY ANNICE [1]

Giles Collins said to his Mother—
   Mother come bind up my head,
And send for the Parson of the Parish,
   For tomorrow I shall be dead.

And if I be dead, as I shall be,
   Before the night do fall,
I'll not be buried in the Churchyard,
   But under Annice's wall.

Lady Annice she sat at her window,
   Mending her of her night coif,
When she saw there as lovely a corpse
   As ever she saw in her life.

What have you there, you six tall men,
   What have you there, said she.
We have the body of Giles Collins,
   Who was a true love to thee.

Set him down, set him down, ye six tall men,
   Set him down upon the Plain;
That I may kiss those rosy lips
   I never may kiss again.

Set him down, set him down, ye six tall men,
   While I look my last on the sun,
For tomorrow before the cock hath crowed,
   Giles Collins and I shall be one.

[1] This ballad has come down in MS. from Betty Duck, nurse to my great-great-grandmother, Mrs. Beckwith, St. Martins-in-Fields, Norwich. According to family letters Betty Duck died a very old woman about 1818. I have not found it in any collection.—L. R. H.

What have you at Giles's burying?
  Very good ale and wine?
You shall have the same tomorrow night,
  At the same hour for mine.

Giles Collins he died upon the eve,
  His fair Lady on the morrow,
Thus may you very well know,
  This couple died for sorrow.

CHAPTER 17

Man's life is like unto a winter's day—
Some break there fast and so depart away;
Others stay dinner, then depart full fed;
The longest age but sups and goes to bed.

JOSEPH HENSHAW, 1631

AFTER I had been in Bungay some few years the Great War come, and
I should like to say that I have been as Patrioch to my King and
Cuntry as the best of them. In 1916 wen they called for Volenteirs, I
Joyned the 5th Suffolk Regment, being one of the first to offer myself for
the Coast Defence Duty. They sent me with a lot of others to Bawdsey,
Sir Quilter's place, and there made me rat Distroyer to all the Troops
round Flextow (Felixtowe) and Walton, though I think I got as much
game as rats.

They were some of the best months I ever spent in my Life, I fairly
enjoyed it. I well rember how the first morning I made the Adgeant
shudder. I had to come and report progress to him after putting in my
traps. I dopped a large rat and put it in with the other dead ones in
my bag, and wile I was counting the rats I pulled the live one out. He
looked at me and told me not to come near his tent any more, and I
did not.

The rats were a proper plage and took a lot of keepen down. It seem to
me that the rat is the most peculiar animile that we have in this Cuntry and
his Habitts take a lot of study befor you can do much with him. I have
Poisoned thousands of these vermin, but the Peculiar thing is that you may
put Poison down for them one time, and they will eate it greedily, and at

other times for no reason you can se they will not touch it. I have always found that they will take poison at the rise of the Moon better than at the full or waste of the Moon.

They are the most fast breeding things on earth, as they will have two lots of young ones in nine weeks, and the young ones will breed again in three months, but as I have said befor Nature go a long way to keep them down, as they have a lot of enimies beside man.

The old male rat will kill and eat the young rats wen they are first born, the same way as they will kill and eat the young mice in a stack. You seldom se many mice were there is a lot of rats in Corn Ricks.

Rats are verry fond of sweet smelling oils such as Rhudon and Cumen and Anerseed, but the best Poison for rats is rock Phosferus, wen you know how to treat it, but that is one of the secrets that I must not give away. I have been told that rats go about in droves, but as I never saw a drove I think that is far fetched. I do believe that the young ones kill the old rats that are diseased, as I have often found them layen about dead badly bitten about the neck and boddy. The stoat always kill with one bite so I have thought the rats themselves kill the more Helples ones among them. Of corse I may be rong as I have never seen them do it, but they are terrible fighters at all time.

Well as to my time Solgeren as I have said it was a good time but nothing much out of the way hapened to me. Of corse we had the ushull stunts. Some times the Bugle would sound the fall in in the middle of the night, and some times the fire bugle would sound. Of corse there was no fire, but the men would have to stand two or three howers wondring what was up. We used to have Concerts and a Cinima and sports and all that sort of thing, and a Gas chamber and we had gas drill wearing masks but bein Rat Destroyer I was out of most of the stunts and all drills and Parades, and there my luck was in.

I had one narrow escape one day wen the sogers had been practising Mills bom throwen with live boms. They threw one that did not explode, and afterwards I found it. I knew how they went and found a lever and hooked it in on the striker, and caried it some time in my hand but I supose I left go of the lever and it begun to fiz.

I knew then that I had only five seconds to go before it burst. I threw the bomb as far as I could and lay down flat on the ground—the bomb exploded and I never got a scratch. I did not have that much luck once out shooting in my Keepering days wen a Gentleman as should have known better went and put eleven shot in my neck, some were got out and some are there now.

I well rember one night we had a terriblle storm which blew all our tents down and left us in a rare muddle. It was more of a Joke afterwards than it was at the time and we made up a rhyme out of that night wich went some thing like this:

> Our Mr. Huddle the Clergyman [1]
> Was in a dreadful Stew
> He had found his sute case gone,
> His Gown and Wiskey too.
>
> Rawle the Rat man struggled hard
> Against the wind and rain
> To find his Boots wich he had lost
> His serch was all in vain.
>
> He had his blanket and his bed—
> But alas no place to lay his head.

I rember the last two verses was some thing like that.

Well, I finished the War there, and in time I come back to Bungay and not so long after I lost my second wife. She had borne me two Children—a Boy and a Girl, she was a good wife to me and I had her for nearly forty years. After I come back the children left home. The girl married a Canadian solger and went to Canadia with him and is there now. As evry one know there was no work for the young men after

[1] He is Rector at St. Mickles now.

the War and so the boy enlisted and is now serving in his Magistey's Army in India. My other son, the son of my first wife, lay some were in France, but he never lived with me, but held by his Grandmother all his life.

I have not said any thing of that side of the war which all had to suffer alike, but there is just one thing I should like to say, about those monuments they have erected to the men that fell in cruell and greedy war. They have put on them 'For God and Cuntry'. The People think wen they read them words that a good God ment that his human beins should be murdered for the lust of Nations, and there Greed. The Bible tell us that he that slay is a murderer, so it is hard to see that there is a Justifacation for that 'For God and Cuntry'. Every man have a right to live they say.

Now they talk about disarment, yet still the cuntrys go on making killing mashiens for the purpose of murdering there fellow men.

It may be I do not hold with monuments. Those things open old wounds and memries in them that lost there near and dear ones although so many years have passed. They have not forgot, and those monuments bring back there tears and the thoughts that would have laid dormant. It is a long while since the war and the edge of there sorows would have worn away if it had not been for them things. Armistice day is quite all rite and a day that should always be rembered and kept, but stand beside the Mothers and wives and se there tears, and then read them words, and I say there is no Justafacation, not for them words.[1]

[1] An opinion voiced by the late Charlotte Mew:

We shall build the Cenotaph; Victory, winged with Peace, winged too at the column's head.
And over the stairway, at the foot—oh! here, leave desolate passionate hands to spread

It was after all that and we were left alone, that my wife fretted and I saw the change in her—she lost all intrest in life and just pined and died. The Doctor said it was hart trubble, and I think it was, but not in the way he ment for I think she died of a broken hart fretting for the children. Now I am left alone and I miss her still as I seam all alone now in my old days, and my work nearly done. But there it is and there was never one like the first one.

Still I must not complain of my lot as I am harty and well and can still work a bit even if I am lame with the Rhumatics, brought on no doubt by exposure in my young days.

I have had one good frend since the days I have been telling about. I met a man that had come home from the war, and him I seamed to take to more than any other man I have ever met. He told me after a bit that he wold like to lern all that I could teach him, and the ins and outs of the Game as I knew it. Well teach him I did, and I found him a verry apt scholler, and consider him one of the Cleverest men that there is on the Job to day, and one of the best Palls.

I have had a verry tryen year this last one and have been onder a verry severe Opperation in Norwich Ospital, and he have stuck to me throw it all and have helped me in evry way that laid in his power, and that is the man that I can eprecate.

I live quite alone now, and I often sit and look back and think of the

Violets, roses, and laurel, with the small sweet twinkling country things,
Speaking so wistfully of other Springs.
       .   .   .

      Only, when all is done and said,
      God is not mocked and neither are the dead.
      For this will stand in our Market-place—
           Who'll sell, who'll buy
           (Will you or I
      Lie to each other with a better grace)?

While looking into every busy whore's and huckster's face
As they drive their bargains. Is this the Face
Of God—some young, piteous, murdered face.

                   'The Cenotaph'
                   From *The Farmer's Bride*

times I had at the Game in them days, and wonder were some of the Boys are that I used to know; gone a long journey most of them I'm thinking. I have exausted my knolidge, Dear Reader, and have no more to rite, so I must bring this life Story to a close as I am thinking of bringing my Life to the same end, only I know I must make myself content to the finish. There is much that I have forgot and a lot that I do not care to rember, as I do not wish to be painted blacker than I am. Do not think too bad of me who ever you are who read this, as they tell me that they are going to make a book of all that I have riten, and begun just to pass the time as I sat thinken.

I always felt I should like to rite my experence of life and Idears, as I have been rather a keen observer of men and there ways and habbitts, but I did not think it wold be of any enterest to any one, as I am not Jack London, Nor a Edger Walice, nor a Sir Rider Haggard—he was a true Gentleman of the Old school. When I get hold of a pen and begin to rite I feel I can go on Just as long as I can hold it. Thoughts come to me that have laid dorment for years—I see old faces and the places that I have forgot, and beleve me though it is so many years ago, the tears come into my eyes wen I write of my first wife, and the things we did wen we were young.

Well, so I have riten it as best I could but I am no scoller. Not that I count myself any the worse for that, it may be verry well for the Upper Classes, or the Middle classes, but for working people lerning is a hinderence and they are best with out it. It lerns the young men and women too much, by that I mean they are educated beyond there classes, and then say—'I am a good scoller, and if I canot find a Job to sute me I will not do any thing at all', and so they drift to crime and Badness.

I consider that if the persons who have to earn there bread as most worken men have to, can read, rite, and sum, and use comon sence, they are fitted for the World at large and fitted to take there place with there fellow men. In my opinion if the men that rule the Cuntry were to pass a law to find work for young beginers fresh from there schooling at

I live quite alone now.

urteen, that would be a great benifit to England. Instead of that they
re goen to throw a class on the cumunity that will never care for any
hing in the shape of hard work. Go to any Labour exchange, se the young
nen there that are practically no use any were. The exchange find them
vork, if they do not like the Job or it is to hard they play there time away
ill the fore man have to sack them. Back they go to the exchange and say
hey could not do the work, sign on, and get there money for play. It
vou 'd be far better if the Minister for Labour said, 'If you will not work
ou must starve'.

I do not pretend to try and lern the Government there Job, but I do
hink if the Government made some provision for young folk to get
vork wen leaven school, we should have a better class of people in the
isen generation, than we have today. The young ones of today are to
roud to work if they can help it, yet look in the papers and se the
undreds of advertisments for servants. The same with the boys, there are
 lot of them here in this town that have left school two or three year, and
ave never done a Job yet as they cannot get any thing to sute them. There
hould be no need for unemployment, in the cuntry there are thousands
f acres of land oncultivated for the want of dranage and land laid down
hat should be growen food for the people. Still I supose there always was
nemployment and always will be, but I dont se that Educating them as
hould be worken with there hands will mend matters. With all the riten
n these matters it seam as if no one can alter it at the present. There is a
ayen goen about that if the Cuntry trubbled more about the pounds and
ounds the Government spend on things that dont matter, instead of so
nuch about the pounds and pounds they spend on the things that do, we
hould all be better off.

I think that they are tryen to lern the comon Generation to be wiser and
re maken them weaker still, any how look at the crimes of today there
eam to be more crime than ever befor. Some people say that it is
nemployment that is causing it, but I do not think so, I beleve it is more
nlightment than any thing else.

Children come into the world to live and it is there birth right. It
said that were God send a child he send a way for him to live, but tha
does not always happen these days. The reports of some of ower schoo
tell us that a verry large number of the children are onder fed and clothe
that is a big shame to our English name.

I wonder wen will the World settle down again—O God let it be son

Well as I have said befor I must bring this book to a close. There is on
thing I should like to say and that is that I have never raided a hen Ro
with all the bad deeds that I have done, I have always had the Idea tha
game was as much mine as any one elses. Did not God say that he gav
all the Beasts and Birds for the use of Man, not the rich alone, and th
Green herbs for the Healing of the Nation.

I envy not the Ritch man's lot, nor the Prince his dream. I have took
fair share of the ritch.

I am well over seventy and am waiting for the last Roll Call. If I ha
my time to come over again I still would be what I have been—
Poacher.

So I remain Gentlemen

The Ex King of the Norfolk Poachers.

THE TRIPLE PLEA

LAW, PHYSIC, and DIVINITY,
Being in dispute could not agree
To settle which among them three
Should have the superiority.

LAW pleads he does preserve men's lands
And all their goods from ravener's hands,
Therefore of right he challenged—he
Should have the superiority.

PHYSIC proscribes receipts for health
(Which men prefer before their wealth)
Therefore of right he challenged—he
Should have the superiority.

Then straight steps up the PRIEST demure,
Who of men's souls hath care and cure;
Therefore of right he challenged—he
Should have the superiority.

If JUDGES end this 'TRIPLE PLEA'
The LAWYER shall bear all the sway.

If UMPIRES then their verdict give,
PHYSICIANS are best of all who live.

If BISHOPS arbitrate the case,
The PRIEST must have the highest place.
181

But if honest sober wise men judge,
Then all the three away may trudge.
But if men fools and knaves will be,
They'll be ass-ridden by all three.

Now if them three cannot agree,
The DEVIL shall ride them three times three.

Obtained in MS. from the landlord of the 'Triple Plea' Inn, Bedingham, Norfolk.

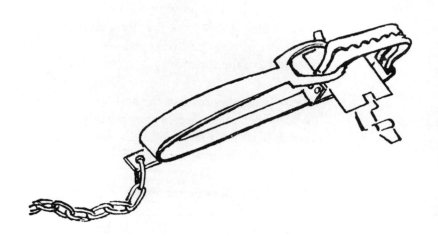

THE END